Praise for Mark David Gerson's Books, Videos & Coaching for Writers

The Voice of the Muse: Answering the Call to Write
Birthing Your Book...Even If You Don't Know What It's About
From Memory to Memoir: Writing the Stories of Your Life
Organic Screenwriting: Writing for Film, Naturally
The Heartful Art of Revision: An Intuitive Guide to Editing
Writer's Block Unblocked! Seven Surefire Ways to Free Up Your Writing and Creative Flow
The Voice of the Muse Companion: Guided Meditations for Writers
Time to Write
Write with Ease
Free Your Characters, Free Your Story!
Journal from the Heart
Write to Heal

Mark David Gerson is the best friend a writer ever had!
LUKE YANKEE – PLAYWRIGHT, SCREENWRITER,
AUTHOR OF "JUST OUTSIDE THE SPOTLIGHT"

One of the most lyrical, spiritual and beautiful books about writing I've ever read.
JULIE ISAAC – AUTHOR & WRITING COACH – LOS ANGELES, CA

Mark David Gerson will make your book-writing dreams a reality. I know. He did it for me!
KAREN HELENE WALKER – AUTHOR OF "THE WISHING STEPS"

A skilled magician, Mark David Gerson is able to draw reluctant words out of even the most blocked writer.
CHRISTOPHER KEMP – CHATHAM, NJ

I owe so much to Mark David! He helped me believe in myself enough to write the book that got two wrongful murder convictions overturned.
ESTELLE BLACKBURN – AUTHOR OF "BROKEN LIVES"

The catalyst I needed to set me free from a nine-year writer's block.
LEILANI LEWIS – KAMUELA, HI

Coaching with Mark David Gerson: Best investment ever!
CHRISTINE FARRIS – DENVER, CO

Without Mark David's inspiration, example and encouragement, I might never have had the courage to publish my book.
NANCY POGUE LATURNER – AUTHOR OF "VOLUNTARY NOMADS"

A highly recommended guide from one of the most creative people around.
WILLIAM C. REICHARD – AUTHOR OF "EVERTIME"

Mark David is a master…one of the great teachers!
REV. MARY OMWAKE – MAUI, HI

More from Mark David Gerson

SELF-HELP & PERSONAL GROWTH

The Way of the Fool: How to Stop Worrying About Life and Start Living It

The Way of the Imperfect Fool: How to Bust the Addiction to Perfection That's Stifling Your Success

The Way of the Abundant Fool: How to Bust Free of "Not Enough" and Break Free into Prosperity

The Way of the Creative Fool: How to Bust Through Your Blocks and Unleash Your Full Creative Potential (coming soon)

The Book of Messages: Writings Inspired by Melchizedek

MEMOIR

Acts of Surrender: A Writer's Memoir

Dialogues with the Divine: Encounters with My Wisest Self

Pilgrimage: A Fool's Journey

FICTION

The MoonQuest, The StarQuest, The SunQuest

The Bard of Bryn Doon

The Lost Horse of Bryn Doon (coming soon!)

The Sorcerer of Bryn Doon (coming soon!)

Sara's Year

After Sara's Year

The Emmeline Papers

WRITER'S BLOCK *unblocked!*

Seven Surefire Ways to
Free Up Your Writing
and Creative Flow

MARK DAVID GERSON

WRITER'S BLOCK UNBLOCKED: SEVEN SUREFIRE WAYS TO
FREE UP YOUR WRITING AND CREATIVE FLOW

Copyright © 2013, 2014, 2022 Mark David Gerson
All rights reserved

No part of this book may be reproduced, stored in a retrieval system or transmitted by any means, electronic, mechanical, photocopying, recording or otherwise, without written permission from the author, except for the inclusion of brief quotations in critical reviews and certain other noncommercial uses permitted by copyright law. And no part of this book may be used or reproduced in any manner for the purpose of training artificial intelligence technologies or systems.

Second Paperback Edition 2022

Published by MDG Media International
www.mdgmediainternational.com

ISBN: 978-1-950189-33-5 (paperback)
ISBN: 978-1-950189-34-2 (ebook)

Cover/Author photographs: Kathleen Messmer
www.kathleenmessmer.com

The Mark David Gerson School of Writing
www.gersonwritingschool.com

More About Mark David Gerson
www.markdavidgerson.com

*Speak from that place in your heart where you are most yourself.
Speak directly, simply, lovingly, gently and without any apologies.
Tell us what you see and want us to see; tell us what you hear and
want us to hear. ... Trust your own heart. The words will come.*

HENRI J.M. NOUWEN

To all the stories that have inspired me and all the storytellers who have told them, to all those who have refused to let fear silence them and to all the voices of creation, wherever they were, are or will be, whatever their medium, I gratefully dedicate this book.

Contents

Opening Words	13
1. Getting Started	19
Why Aren't You Writing?	21
How to Use This Book	23
Preparing to Flow Forward	25
Guided Meditations	27
2. Flowing Forward	29
The Myth of Writer's Block	31
Floating Freely on the Muse Stream	33
Seven Surefire Ways to Navigate the Muse Stream	37
3. The Muse Stream and You	41
The Keys to Your Creative Flow	43
Seventy Keys to Unlock Your Muse Stream	45
The Word Tree	49
Find Your Key: Two Quick Meditations	51
After You've Written	55
The Truth About Your Muse	57
Meet Your Muse: A Guided Meditation	59
4. 12½ "Rules" for Freeing Up Your Creative Flow	63
The "Rules"	65
1. There Are No Rules	67
I Did It My Way	67
2. Get Out of Your Own Way	71
Writing into Uncharted Territory	71
3. Leap into the Void...and Trust	75

Your Story Is Smarter Than You Are	75
Toss Out the Itinerary	76
4. Listen...and Always Go with First Thoughts	79
The Wisdom of First Thoughts	79
5. Surrender to the Muse Stream	81
Writing into the Chaos	81
If the Muse Stream Is Good Enough for Francis Ford Coppola, It's Good Enough for You!	82
Relax. It's Only Your First Draft...	84
6. Be In the Moment	87
One Step at a Time...One Word at a Time	87
Grounded in the Moment: A Guided Meditation	89
7. Go for the Jugular	93
"Walk the Earth Naked, Clothed Only in Your Truth"	93
The Mask: A Guided Meditation	96
8. Love Yourself and Your Words	101
Say "*No*" to Judgment	101
Let Judgment Go...and Let Your Story Flow: A Guided Meditation	103
9. Strip Off Your Straitjackets	107
Revelations on the Muse Stream	107
It's All About Trust	108
The Market Is Fickle: Ignore Today's Trends	110
10. Write	111
Just Do It!	111
11. Set Yourself Up for Success	113
The Secret to Healthy Goal-Setting	113
Celebrate Every Success	114
Gold Stars	116
12. Empower Yourself	117
The Past is Passed. Let It Go.	117
Your Words. Your Creative Journey.	118
12½. There Are No Rules	121
I Did It My Way...and It Paid Off!	121

5. Your Writer's Vision — 123

- What's Your Vision? — 125
- My Vision — 127
- Visioning Your Story — 129
- Your Vision Quest: A Guided Meditation — 131
- How to Use Your Vision Statement — 137

6. Busted: Seven Common Writers' Myths — 139

- The Myths — 141
- 1. "I'm Blocked" — 143
- 2. "I'm Easily Distracted" — 145
  - Seven Common Excuses for Delaying (or Avoiding) Writing — 145
  - Seven Tips for Minimizing Distraction and Procrastination — 146
  - Put Away Your Journal — 149
  - Distraction Happens — 150
- 3. "I Don't Have Time To Write" — 153
  - Where Does the Time Go? — 153
  - How I Found the Time to Write — 155
  - Now Is the Time to Write — 156
  - How Much Did You Write? — 157
- 4. "I Never Finish Anything I Start" — 159
  - The Breath of Creativity — 159
- 5. "I Don't Know How to Start or End" — 161
  - Your Story Is Waiting for You — 161
- 6. "I Don't Know Anything About…" — 163
  - Write What You Know…If You Dare — 163
- 7. "I'm Not Good Enough" — 167
  - You Are Good Enough — 167
  - A Good Writer Is… — 169

7. Busted: Seven Common Writer's Block Myths — 171

- The Myths — 173
- 1. "I Have Writer's Block" — 175

There Is No Writer's Block	*175*
2. "Writer's Block Means I Have Nothing Creative, Original or Meaningful to Say"	*177*
Your Story, Your Way	*177*
Creations of the Heart	*179*
3. "Writer's Block Means I'm Lazy"	*181*
The Miracle of the Seed	*181*
4. "Writer's Block Means I'm Not Disciplined"	*185*
Into the Heart of Discipline	*185*
5. "Writer's Block Means I'm Not Really a Writer"	*189*
Kafka Nearly Couldn't	*189*
Tolstoy's Complaint	*190*
6. "Writer's Block Means I'm a Failure…"	*191*
I Believe in You	*191*
Never Give Up!	*192*
"I Am a Writer. Period."	*192*
7. "I Have Writer's Block"	*195*
The Butterfly: A Guided Meditation	*195*
8. Get Unblocked! Seven Surefire Solutions	**199**
Seven Surefire Solutions	*201*
1. Say "No" to Fear	*203*
Write the Fear: A Guided Meditation	*203*
Making Friends with Your Inner Critic	*204*
Talk to Your Block	*206*
Making Friends with Your Inner Critic: A Guided Meditation	*207*
Risky Writing	*210*
Say "No" to Shame	*211*
2. Abandon Control	*213*
It's Time to Let Go	*213*
Whose Story Is It?	*214*
Embrace the Chaos	*216*
Trickster Tales	*218*
It's All in Order…Even When It Isn't	*219*
3. Rethink Your Routines	*221*

Seven Surefire Ways to Rethink Your Writing Routines	222
Seven Surefire Tools for Transition	225
4. Strive for Excellence, Not Perfection	231
Embrace Imperfection	231
The Pain of Perfection	234
As Good as It Gets	235
5. Learn to Tell the Write Time	237
It Isn't Always Time to Write	237
6. Rekindle Your Passion	239
Is Your Write Idea the Right Idea for You?	239
7. Say "Yes" to You	241
Know Thyself	241
Dare to Create. Dare to Write.	242
Say "Yes" to Your Muse: A Guided Meditation	243

9. The Soul of Creation — 245

Pre-Conception	247
Listen for the Voice of Your Muse	249
The Soul of Creation: A Guided Meditation	251
A Story is Born	253
Birthing Your Story: A Guided Journey	255

10. Other Perspectives — 259

Sympathetic Vibrations	261
The Seven Be's of Empowered Feedback	263
The Seven Be's of Compassionate Feedback	267
Creative Connection	269

11. On Rejection — 273

Feeling Rejected? Don't Be Dejected	275
Still Dejected? Here Are More of the Infamously Rejected	277
When You're Rejected...	281
When the Critics Come Knocking...	285

    See the Perfection in All Things: A Guided Meditation *287*

12. Be the Writer You Are   291

    Acts of Commitment *293*
    The Gift of Your Words *295*
    Heartful Acts of Revolution *297*
    Say What? *299*
    When Was the Last Time You Told Your Story? *303*
    The Spirit and Essence of Your Story: A Guided
        Meditation *305*

13. The Courage to Create   309

    Write to Connect *311*
    Write from the Heart: A Guided Meditation *313*
    Living the Creative Life *317*
        12½ "Rules" for Living a Creative Life *317*
    Remember Who You Are *323*
    Resistance is Futile *325*
    Write, Now *327*
    Trust. Let Go. Leap. *329*
    You Are a Writer: A Guided Meditation *331*

14. Before You Go…   333

    Leaps of Faith *335*
    It's Time to Live the Dream: A Guided Meditation *337*

Endings and Beginnings   339

Share the Journey   343

Gratitude   345

Opening Words

Never let the fear of striking out keep you
from playing the game.
BABE RUTH

If you hear a voice within you say "you cannot paint,"
then by all means paint, and that voice will be silenced.
VINCENT VAN GOGH

It's October 2012, a few days after my birthday, and I'm on the phone with Aalia, my former wife and still a good friend.

"You have so much terrific material on writing and creativity," she says, "you should write a series of books on the subject, as companions to *The Voice of the Muse*. Ebooks," she adds, "because you could probably write one and get it up in a few weeks."

I'm not opposed to Aalia's suggestion. But nor do I pay much attention to it. I'm immersed in another round of revisions to my *Q'ntana* fantasy books and screenplays. Who has time to take on another project?

Months pass, and I think nothing more about it.

It's now late March 2013. I have completed all my *Q'ntana* final drafts and believe I have brought to completion the nineteen-year odyssey that began when *The MoonQuest*'s first words spilled unexpectedly out of me during a workshop I was facilitating. The last thing I am thinking about is another writing project.

Then I remember Aalia's words. I dismiss them at first, even as I recognize not only their rightness but the track record of their messenger, clearly one of my Muse's most reliable envoys.

We were living in Hawaii and still married when Aalia first urged me to put together a book on writing. It was also her idea to combine the book with a recording of guided meditations for writers. And when I had written an early version, it was she who came up with the title, *The Voice of the Muse: Answering the Call to Write*.

Aalia's direct line to my Muse is also, in part, responsible for the *Q'ntana* movies. It was during another phone call with her, before *The MoonQuest* was published, that she urged me to try my hand at a screenplay adaptation of my fantasy novel. It took several months and a few nudges before I surrendered to that notion.

Within days of remembering all this, I surrender again — this time to the book that almost immediately titles itself *Writer's Block*

Unblocked! Seven Surefire Ways to Free Up Your Writing and Creative Flow and that gushes out of me with dizzying speed.

I begin by sketching out some book cover ideas and start writing the following day. Although the writing flows easily (no writer's block there!), I am skeptical about the completion date I'm intuiting. It's less than three weeks away and seems ridiculously unrealistic. In the end, I finish ahead of schedule, in sixteen days. The original ebook edition is available for sale a few days later.

When I wrote my first draft of *The SunQuest* novel in three weeks, I was astounded. I had never written anything that quickly before. Now this: Sixteen days from surrender through multiple drafts and all the way to completion. I'm stunned...and, of course, grateful.

I am grateful, too, to Aalia for continuing to channel the Ideas Division of MDG's Muse, Inc. I'm more grateful still for the precepts and philosophies in this and all my books — ways of writing and living that have brought me, once more, to the place of surrender where a book like this could write itself through me so quickly and painlessly.

Writer's Block Unblocked may have taken me only sixteen days to write, but it took me more than sixteen years to reach the place of surrender where those sixteen days could be possible.

In the end, surrender is what this book is about. It's what all my books, talks, coaching and workshops are about. It's what my life is about. It's about trusting in the superior wisdom of the story we are living as much as the story we are writing, and doing our imperfect best to get out of our own way so that those stories can flow through us.

May *Writer's Block Unblocked* help you rediscover that same place of surrender within yourself, and may your stories always flow through you naturally, effortlessly and with ease.

Mark David Gerson
Albuquerque, New Mexico
December 2013

Why a New Edition?

When I began work on this second edition of *Writer's Block Unblocked*, my plan was to add a few new exercises and guided meditations, flesh out some of the other text and give it a new cover. I conceived it as a minor update, one that would take no more than a few weeks to pull together. At the time, I was already seven chapters into a new novel, a fifth book in my *Legend of Q'ntana* fantasy series, and I didn't want another major project to impede my momentum.

As you move through *Writer's Block Unblocked*, however, it won't take you long to discover that our stories, whatever form they take, are not only smarter than we are, they're also tricksters. So I should have known better, especially as one of the so-called "rules" for writing in another of my books says, "your book is boss." (You'll discover why "rules" is always in quotation marks in Section 4.)

The original edition of *Writer's Block Unblocked* was conceived as a companion to what then was my only book for writers, *The Voice of the Muse: Answering the Call to Write*. But once I began rereading it for my "minor update," I quickly realized that the new edition already had a voice, a loud one that wasn't shy about making its demands known. It would *not* be some other book's sidekick. It would stand as an equal alongside my other books for writers.

If I have learned anything through more than three decades of writing, it's that my stories know best. Always. If *Writer's Block Unblocked* said it needed a comprehensive overhaul, then a comprehensive overhaul it would get.

For this revised edition, I have added new exercises and meditations, expanded the book's inspirational and motivational content and reorganized some of the original material for clarity and better flow. And I have delved beneath writer's block to touch on some of the life issues that are at the root of all barriers to creative expression. The result is an edition that's more than twice the size of its predecessor and, I hope, at least twice as effective.

I'm counting on it being at least twice as effective for me, too, as I return to work on that novel of mine, having now completed a quick (if not as quick as I'd planned) refresher on creative flow through *Writer's Block Unblocked*.

May it be equally effective for you as, through these pages, you unleash your creative potential and set your stories free.

Mark David Gerson
Sedona, Arizona
June 2022

1. Getting Started

There is no greater agony than bearing
an untold story inside you.
ZORA NEALE HURSTON

One day you finally knew
what you had to do, and began,
though the voices around you
kept shouting their bad advice...
MARY OLIVER

Why Aren't You Writing?

What brought you to this book, to this page? Why are you reading my words instead of writing your own? What is holding you back?

Do you ask yourself these questions as you stare at a blank notepad, gripping your pen so tightly that your knuckles have turned white? Or are your eyes fixed on a screen that is empty but for a cursor that blinks back at you with compassionless recrimination? Perhaps your fingers are frozen over your keyboard, uncertain which letters to strike...not knowing which words to set down...which might be the *right* words to set down.

Or have you not even made it to your computer, mobile device or notepad? Do they sit sequestered in another room, physically separate but still calling to you through closed doors?

Do you have a project that you have not been able to start? Have you begun but find yourself stuck partway through or close to completion but unable to finish? Or do you feel a powerful call to write but don't know *what* to write?

Maybe the door to your writing studio is open and the idea is clear in your mind, but procrastination or distraction keep you from it. Even if you're stronger than those, obligation can easily get in your way...to family, friends, colleagues and others close to you. Or to your school, day job or volunteer commitments.

Whatever brought you to this page, chances are you're not writing, you're not writing what you desire to be writing or you're not writing with the discipline and commitment that lead to completion.

It's time to change all that.

It's time to journey into the heart of your passion and creativity.

It's time to turn the page and begin.

How to Use This Book

There are no rules, as you will read in Section 4. There is no right way and no wrong way. There is only the way that works for you, today. Given that, I could hardly insist you begin *Writer's Block Unblocked* on page 1 and continue straight through to the end. After all, I didn't write it that way. Why should I insist you read it that way?

Rather, as I do with all my books for writers, I encourage you to use this book however you feel called to. While the sections are presented in an intentional sequence that will work perfectly for many of you, I know — and urge you to trust — that whichever page you open to will present the inspirational nugget or exercise perfectly suited to your needs of the moment. All I ask is that, however you journey through this book, you visit the first two chapters of the next section early in your travels. They, along with Section 4's "12½ 'Rules' for Freeing Up Your Creative Flow" present the foundational philosophy upon which the rest of the book is based.

Consider, too, keeping a journal dedicated to your explorations. Not only will it keep you writing, a *Writer's Block Unblocked* journal can be the place where you observe, consider and resolve whatever issues have carried you to these pages and where you do the book's exercises, at least those unrelated to a specific project.

Your *Writer's Block Unblocked* journal can be a dedicated journal, or you can integrate it into an existing journal. It can be a physical book or a journal you keep on your computer or mobile device, either using your regular writing application or a journaling app. Regardless, have your *Writer's Block Unblocked* journal close at hand whenever you work with this book.

Are you ready to flow forward into your creative reawakening? Open your *Writer's Block Unblocked* journal and let's get started.

Preparing to Flow Forward

Where are you now? Where are you now in your writing? In your life? Where are you *not* in your writing? In your life?

What does writer's block mean to you? How has it shown up for you? What is writer's block preventing you from starting? From finishing? From accomplishing?

What brought you to this book...to this question, to this page? What prompted you to start this book today?

What do you want from this book? What are your desires? Your hopes? Your expectations? Your preferences?

Where would you like to be on the final page that you aren't now? In your writing? In your life?

Close your eyes and let those questions roll around in your mind. Let them roll around in your heart. Don't overthink them. Don't think about them at all. Feel them. Feel through them. Breathe into them. Meditate on them. Let them sit silently within you for five minutes or ten or twenty — as long as it takes to get out of your head and into the true heart of the matter...into the kind of clarity that derives only from the heart.

When you feel ready, but only then, gently open your eyes and your *Writer's Block Unblocked* journal and jot down some notes about what you sensed and felt...about what you saw and heard. Record those desires, those expectations, those preferences, those sensations. Let it be a few words, a few sentences or a few pages. Let it be whatever you need it to be. Let it express whatever you opened this book seeking.

When you're finished, turn to a fresh page in your journal and forget about this opening exercise until later. Much later. Until you have finished the book.

What's next? You have hoisted your sail. Now it's time to let the wings of your desire, the winds of your creativity and the waves of the Muse Stream carry you to your destination. What's a Muse Stream? I'll have more to say about that in Section 2. But first...

Guided Meditations

Whenever I facilitate a workshop, I nearly always incorporate a guided journey as part of the experience. It's an opportunity for writers to, in a sense, lose their mind and find their heart — the heart of a particular project and the heart of their creative process.

For that reason, I have included fourteen full-length guided meditations and several shorter ones in *Writer's Block Unblocked*. Among their other purposes, these immersive experiences will help you...

- unblock stagnant creative flow
- free yourself from harsh self-judgment
- tame your inner critic
- connect you with the spirit and essence of your story, even if you're not yet sure what that story is
- discover your vision for your writing and your vision for yourself as the writer you are
- affirm your creative power

How to Use a Guided Meditation

Here are some options...

- Record it yourself for playback (record it into your phone's voice memos app for easy access).
- Have a friend or writing partner read the meditation to you, then return the favor.
- Get into a quiet place/inner space, set your music player for five to forty-five minutes of contemplative music or nature sounds (depending on the length of the exercise) and read the meditation slowly and receptively, following its directions and suggestions.

If you prefer a professionally guided approach, I have recorded eight of the meditations (along with two others not included in this book) on my album *The Voice of the Muse Companion: Guided Meditations for Writers*.

- "Meet Your Muse" (Section 3: "The Muse Stream and You")
- "Let Judgment Go…and Let Your Story Flow" (Section 4: "12½ 'Rules' for Freeing up Creative Your Flow")
- "Your Vision Quest" (Section 5: "Your Writer's Vision")
- "The Butterfly" (Section 7: "Busted: Seven Common Writer's Block Myths")
- "Making Friends with Your Inner Critic"; on the recording it's titled "Taming Your Critic" (Section 8: "Get Unblocked! Seven Surefire Solutions")
- "The Soul of Creation" (Section 9: "The Soul of Creation")
- "Write from the Heart" (Section 13: "The Courage to Create")
- "You Are a Writer" (Section 13: "The Courage to Create")

The *Voice of the Muse Companion* album also includes a version of my "12½ 'Rules' for Freeing Up Creative Your Flow" (Section 4), perfect for those moments when you need an inspirational boost.

How to Access the Recorded Meditations

- Stream all but "Vision Quest" for free as a subscriber to Apple Music, YouTube Music or Amazon Music Unlimited. Or download those individual tracks from Amazon or Apple Music. The two-part "Your Vision Quest" meditation is available only on *The Voice of the Muse Companion* album, not as a standalone track.
- Experience a free video version of "You Are a Writer" and an abridged version of "Let Judgment Go" on my YouTube channel[1].
- Download the complete *Voice of the Muse Companion* album from my website[2] or from Apple Music, Amazon or CD Baby.

---

[1] www.youtube.com/markdavidgerson
[2] www.markdavidgerson.com/books

2. *Flowing Forward*

Writing is an act of faith, nothing else.
E.B. Wϰite

I learned a long time ago to trust my intuition.
Bob Dylan

The Myth of Writer's Block

You don't have to experience writer's block. Ever. You don't have to sweat over the blank page. You don't have to chew your pencil (or fingernails) to the nub. You don't have to wonder where the next word is coming from.

Writer's block is a myth — not because you won't ever feel stuck but because there is no reason for you ever to stay stuck.

Do you wonder where your next breath is coming from? Unless you suffer from some sort of respiratory disease, you rarely think about your breath. You assume it will come, and it does. One breath, then another... then another.

It comes because you let it. It comes because you don't get in its way. It comes because you're not thinking about it or worrying about it.

Words can be like that too.

When you trust in your story, in its inherent wisdom, the words always come. The words always come because they are already there. They're there because, in some sense, your story already exists.

It exists in the same invisible realm in which your dreams, visions and ideas exist. And when you believe in that existence, when you trust in that existence, you will never lack the words your story needs for its expression.

"Fine words," I hear you say. "But I'm still stuck."

You may be stuck, but you are not blocked. And you certainly have not lost your creative ability.

You cannot lose something that's an innate part of you, that's an innate part of everyone. Creativity is as natural as breathing and as long as you're breathing, you can write.

So how do you get to that place where your story's words flow as effortlessly as your breath? By writing on the Muse Stream.

What's a Muse Stream? Read on and I'll tell you.

Floating Freely on the Muse Stream

Whether you're journaling, writing for personal growth or with the goal of creating a book, short story, song, poem, essay, dissertation, stage play, screenplay or other project destined for the public, the core technique I use and teach is what I call "writing on the Muse Stream." I call it the Muse Stream because I believe that when we surrender to our Muse, creativity pours through us as effortlessly as water in a free-flowing stream.

Here's how it works: Write the first thing that comes into your head, then keep going, without stopping.

Keep going even if you have no clear idea what to write or where the writing will take you.

Keep going even if the writing takes you in unexpected or uncomfortable directions.

Keep going especially if the writing takes you in unexpected or uncomfortable directions.

Keep going, and don't stop for *any* reason.

Here are seven reasons why you might consider stopping. Don't do it.

1. You've noticed or been alerted to a typo or misspelled word, a punctuation error or a problem with your grammar. Don't stop to make corrections. Better yet, if your computer or mobile device is set for spellcheck, autocorrect or grammar-check, disable those features while you compose your first draft. At the very least, mute all notifications. Not only do you want to avoid distraction, you want to avoid being alerted to anything that might require correction, to anything that might pull you out of your creative flow. *Keep going.*

2. You can't think of the word you're looking for, or a word you've written isn't quite right. Don't stop to grope for the word or to consult a thesaurus, online or off. Instead, leave a blank space or write *xxxx*. If you don't like the word you've just written, convert

it to all caps, bold it or underline it, or change its color, whichever is quickest and easiest. That way you'll know to deal with it in your next draft. Writing longhand? Circle the problem word. *Keep going.*

3. You want to make sure that what you wrote yesterday or last week is good enough. Don't stop to read, edit or rewrite what's already on the page. Don't stop to look back. Keep moving forward. *Keep going.*

4. You worry that what you're writing isn't making sense or is inconsistent, illogical, irrelevant or repetitive. You worry that your paragraphs or chapters are too long or too short. Or you worry that other aspects of your work's structure or format are all wrong, a common source of anxiety for screenwriters. Don't stop to think or worry about any of that. If there are issues, address them in subsequent drafts. That's what those drafts are for. *Keep going.*

5. You feel compelled to monitor your progress. "What's my word count?" "What's my page count?" "Have I written enough today... this week...this month...on this draft?" As long as you're moving forward, you're making all the progress you need to be making. Stop counting. Keep writing. *Keep going.*

6. You're convinced you can't continue until you can accurately describe a 1952 Hudson Hornet for the scene you're writing, until you have the precise dates of the first Soviet space mission, or until you get clarity about some other vital fact or detail. You *can* continue. Whatever your perceived research gap, don't let it dam up your Muse Stream. Make a note about the needed information, set aside separate, *non-writing* time for research, and *keep going.*

7. You're judging, criticizing or second-guessing what you have already written or what you sense is coming next. Or you worry how your mother, father, child, best friend or significant other will react to what you're writing. Don't stop to consider the impact of your words. Not in your early drafts. And don't stop to censor. *Keep going.*

Writing on the Muse Stream means trusting that the words will flow from you freely, if you let them...that the next word will come as effortlessly as your next breath, if you allow it to be so.

Writing on the Muse Stream prevents your head from getting in the way of your heart and stops your personality mind from blocking the free flow of your authentic, uncensored, wisest and most creative expression.

Writing on the Muse Stream separates your Creator and Editor personas and allows each to do its best job in its right time.

Writing on the Muse Stream prevents that inner critic we all carry from judging your output and censoring your flow.

Writing on the Muse Stream gets your first thoughts and most original ideas onto the page where they belong. And it does so naturally, spontaneously and *without struggle.*

Whenever you're writing, whatever you're writing, allow your pen to keep flowing across the page or your fingers to continue dancing across the keyboard. Don't stop for *any* reason.

"But I'll freeze up," you say. "What do I do when no words are there? How do I keep writing if nothing is coming?" Yes, you may encounter shoals in your Muse Stream. We all do. But shoals are not impenetrable dams, and there are always ways to navigate through and past them. Surefire ways. Discover seven in the next chapter.

Seven Surefire Ways to Navigate the Muse Stream

If you get stuck, and you will — we all do — do whatever it takes to keep your pen moving or your fingers typing. This alone will carry you through and past all perceived blocks.

Here's the biggest secret of this book: When the words don't want to come, it doesn't matter what you write, even if it's gibberish or unrelated to the project at hand. It may feel foolish in the moment, but it's guaranteed to carry you through and past most fear and hesitation. And before you know it, you'll be back in a free and easy flow.

What about those extraneous, off-topic words, sentences, paragraphs or pages that helped get you back on track? Edit them out in a future draft...although you may discover some to be surprisingly relevant.

Here are those seven surefire ways to keep the words flowing. Until you're certain you'll remember them, revisit them before starting any of this book's exercises...or any Muse Stream writing.

1. Repeat

Repetition is a powerful tool for freeing your flow from your mind's fearful grasp. Repeat anything to keep your pen moving or your fingers typing: the previous word or sentence, your starting word or sentence, or anything at all, even if it's "I don't know what to write" or "This is stupid" or "This book is dumb." Continue repeating your word, phrase or sentence until your flow opens up again. And it will. Don't judge the repeated words or phrases. Some, as I noted above, may end up as an integral part of the final work. You will discard others in later drafts.

2. Free-Associate

Let one word trigger the next — whatever leaps to mind, however silly and illogical. Use the last word you wrote and free-associate from that. Was the last word "chair"? From chair, I free-associate arm ... *leg ... foot ... toe ... tow ... truck ... muck ... duck ... quack ... flack ... back ... front ... side ... sighed ... cried ... spied ...* and on and on. Keep at it until the flow returns. It always does.

3. Switch Languages

If you're fluent enough in another language, change over to it for a while. This can be especially helpful if English isn't your first language and you find yourself struggling for an English term.

4. Write Your Breath

The best way to remain present and in the flow is through your breath. Write, "I am breathing in" as you inhale and "I am breathing out" as you exhale. Keep repeating the pair of sentences and keep matching your breath with what you're writing until your flow returns. And it will. Your breath may also help you retrieve words and images from the deepest wells of your unconscious mind, which is the realm of your Muse.

5. Write Blind

Close your eyes, breathe deeply and write without watching your hand, screen or notepad. Removing your attention from the external act of writing and placing it on your breath will carry you inward, away from the source of your anxiety and toward the source of your words and story. Remember to breathe, remember to turn your page if you're writing longhand and, if you're using a traditional keyboard, remember to keep feeling for the notches on the *F* and *J* keys.

Caveat: Proceed with caution. It's easy when writing longhand to write over what you have already written, and when on a computer or mobile device to hit the wrong keys. I've done both. I once handwrote several pages on top of each other because I was so in the flow that I forgot to turn the page. There was also one writing session where I typed several pages in a (fortunately decipherable) "code," when one hand strayed a single key to the right.

6. Get Whimsical

Make up words…words that sound funny…words that sound weird…words that don't exist in any known dictionary. Make one up, write it down…then another…then another…then another. This playful act tricks your inner censor into dropping its guard. Soon, nonsense words will become Muse-sense words and your flow will resume. Alternatively, repeat something like *la-la-la-la*.

If you're writing longhand, here's more whimsy… Turn your page sideways or upside down. Or start writing in a spiral or around the edges of the page. Or exchange your conventional black or blue ballpoint or roller ball for a brightly colored pen, pencil or marker or for a crayon. Such startling changes work to stun your censorious mind and free up your flow. (The final exercise in Section 4 uses a variation of this technique.)

7. Doodle

If all else fails and you're writing longhand, draw or doodle. Frankly, it doesn't matter what you do, as long as you keep the ink flowing onto your page. Before long, squiggles will make way for words, words will form into sentences and you will forget that you ever felt stuck.

∫ ∫ ∫

Now that you know what a Muse Stream is and how and why it works, it's time to experience it for yourself. Turn the page and let's see it in action.

3. The Muse Stream and You

When you have an important story to tell, the words you need
seem to come of their own accord.
J.A. JANCE

One of the things I had to learn as a writer was to trust
the act of writing. To put myself in the position
of writing to find out what I was writing.
E.L. DOCTOROW

The Keys to Your Creative Flow

You're probably familiar with the term "keyword" in its search or indexing context. The *New Oxford American Dictionary*, however, also defines it as "a word or concept of great significance," and it's that definition that is most relevant here. After all, what could be more significant than the word or phrase that launches your writing journey and propels it forward? That word or phrase is the "key" that unlocks the dam blocking your Muse Stream and releases the natural free-flow of your creativity. Your *keyword*.

The keyword or key phrase you choose (or that chooses you) is less important than the act of surrender it represents because once you surrender to the journey, the perfect words will always emerge, regardless of how you begin. At the same time, keywords and key phrases offer not only convenient starting points but can trick your logical, fearful or judgmental mind into abandoning control.

What follows is a series of exercises designed to help you practice writing on the Muse Stream using a keyword or key phrase. Return to them whenever you need a Muse Stream refresher or any time your creativity needs a jump-start.

¶ *Read "After You've Written," later in this section, before you read over any of your writing from the exercises in this section.*

TRY THIS

Get a giant piece of poster board and, in big, fat, bold, bright letters, write: WRITE! DON'T THINK!! Tape the sign over your computer or writing space so that it's always visible when you're writing.

Seventy Keys to Unlock Your Muse Stream

Pick a word or phrase from the list below using any of the following four methods to make your selection:

- Pick a word at random.
- Close your eyes and let your finger drop to a word or phrase.
- Close your eyes, choose a number between one and seventy, and let that number direct you to your keyword or key phrase.
- Run through the list in order, one word or phrase per writing session.

Don't hesitate to play with the list: Add words, alter or combine phrases, turn positive statements into negatives, change genders/tenses or make any other adjustments you feel like making. Creativity is about having fun…so have fun!

Once you pick your keyword or key phrase, jot it down, then continue on the Muse Stream. Write without thinking, without stopping, without judging and without censoring. Let the words, sentences and paragraphs emerge naturally. Don't worry where or whether they will fit into a story or other writing project. Your job right now isn't to figure anything out. Your job is to dive in and write.

Set a timer for twenty or thirty minutes the first few times you use this list. Setting a timer forces you to keep going when you feel you can't and gives you an opportunity to practice some or all of the techniques in "Seven Surefire Ways to Navigate the Muse Stream" (Section 2).

The List

1. Ocean
2. I don't know...
3. I wish I knew...
4. We're best enemies...
5. When I write I... / When I don't write I...
6. When I fell out of/into the airplane, I...
7. Chocolate
8. I embrace...
9. I reject...
10. The window shattered and...
11. The vampire...
12. If I could write any story, it would be about...
13. If only I had/hadn't...
14. Summer is/was...
15. The full moons...
16. Success means...
17. I love/hate writing because...
18. Failure means...
19. I remember...
20. I forget...
21. I am/am not a writer because...
22. "Shall we dance?"
23. I feel/don't feel/can't feel...
24. The quick brown fox...
25. Once/twice upon a time...
26. The day I was born, I...
27. Sometimes I wish...
28. My mother/father always told me to/never to...
29. The wind tasted like...
30. The clouds sounded like...
31. Black
32. I wish she/he/they had never...
33. I feel blocked because...
34. I trust...
35. "They're coming for me!"
36. Raspberries
37. The door slammed shut...
38. Twinkle, twinkle, little...
39. I write to...
40. When I was ninety...
41. When I turn ninety...
42. Now that I'm ninety...
43. When I looked down/up the well, I saw...
44. Money
45. I'm the world's worst writer because...
46. "You're not making any sense!"
47. Sex

48. I close my eyes and see...
49. I open my heart and know...
50. The curtain rose and...
51. I was born to...
52. I desire...
53. Leap of faith
54. I love... / I hate...
55. Mars
56. My Muse says...
57. I trust/don't trust...
58. I first felt blocked when...
59. It was a dark and stormy planet...
60. Eighty-eight cats
61. Creation
62. Word
63. The door opened...
64. Truth
65. Deadlines
66. It was the winter of my best contentment...
67. The end.
68. After the end...
69. The beginning...
70. I am the best writer in the world!

The Word Tree

A Word Tree[1] is a nonlinear type of outline, designed to open your mind to fresh ideas and new possibilities. Here's how to plant your own.

In the center of a large piece of blank, unlined paper, print "My Story," then draw a circle around it. This is the trunk of your Word Tree.

By the way, I use the word "story" here and throughout this book in its broadest sense, to encompass all that you would write — fiction or nonfiction...novel, stage play or screenplay...essay, short story, poem, song or vignette. Everything you write, everything you experience, everything you share: It's all story.

With "My Story" in the center of your page as the trunk of your Word Tree, write the first word or phrase that leaps to mind, without stopping to think, analyze, criticize, second-guess or judge. It doesn't have to have any logical connection to "My Story" or to anything that you think you might want to write...or to anything at all.

Now, circle your new word, link it with a line to "My Story" and continue — by quickly writing, circling and linking the words triggered by each new association. See each circled word or phrase as a leaf and each connecting line as a branch in this Word Tree you are growing.

Continue free-associating in this way until you feel complete with a particular branch. Then either return to "My Story" or begin a new branch from any word or phrase you have already jotted down. Keep going for five, ten or fifteen minutes, or until you have a sense that your Word Tree has grown to maturity.

Once your Word Tree is complete, scan the page — again, not with your critical or analytical mind. Do it instead from an open, intuitive, free-flowing place.

As you do, let a word or phrase bubble up from your unconscious. It

---

[1] The Word Tree is adapted from the clustering technique developed and popularized by Gabriele Lusser Rico in her landmark book, *Writing the Natural Way* (Tarcher/Penguin, 1983, 2002).

could be a word or phrase that jumps out at you from the Word Tree, or it could be something else altogether. Whatever it is, jot it down and let it be your keyword or key phrase, the kickoff to an experience of writing on the Muse Stream.

Write on the Muse Stream for twenty to thirty minutes; set a timer should that prove helpful. Remember to write without pausing to correct spelling, punctuation or grammar or to hunt for the "right" word. Remember, too, that if you feel stuck, you can use the repetition, free-association, breathing or whimsy tips in "Seven Surefire Ways to Navigate the Muse Stream" (Section 2) to reinitiate the flow.

When your time is up, set your writing aside for at least an hour. Take a walk or do something else unrelated to writing. When you feel able to look at what you have written uncritically and without judgment, read it — with an open heart and mind — and see what it tells you about your story, yourself or both. If you're not one hundred percent certain that you can read it uncritically and without judgment, skip to "After You've Written," later in this section, before looking at it. While this exercise is not designed to produce direct content, it may.

Find Your Key

Two Quick Meditations

Key Meditation #1

Have any book or other printed text in front of you before you start.

Allow at least 20 minutes for this meditation and for the writing experience that flows from it.

Set a timer for twenty or thirty minutes, then close your eyes and take a few deep breaths. As you relax into your breath, feel the stress of your day melt away. Let your shoulders drop, and let all the weight of responsibility and obligation we too often feel dissolve on your breath.

With your eyes still shut, reach for the book you have chosen for this exercise and either open it at random or let your intuition guide you to the perfect page. Now, let your index finger drop to somewhere on the page. Again, use your intuition or let it be a random experience.

Once your finger has found its spot, open your eyes, note the word or phrase it's pointing to, and let that be the word or phrase that launches your creative journey on the Muse Stream. Don't judge or second-guess it. Don't censor or reject it. Whatever it is, trust that it's the best possible word or phrase, and start writing.

Continue writing until the timer goes off...longer, if you feel like it. Remember to write without stopping, for any reason. That means no pauses to edit, make corrections, search for the right word or read over what you've written.

If you feel yourself losing momentum, repeat the last word or sentence you wrote or return to your keyword or opening sentence. Or free-associate. If you feel your center straying or your mind taking charge, return your focus to your breath.

Remember, this is not about a perfect finished draft. It may not even be about writing that makes sense to your conscious mind. This is about floating on the Muse Stream and discovering how effortless creative flow can be.

Key Meditation #2

You needn't rely on a book, a list or any other external source to come up with the keyword or key phrase that launches your Muse Stream journey. This exercise is an easy way to conjure up your own.

Remember, the word or phrase that comes to you, whatever it is, is merely a jumping-off point and may have little or nothing to do with your final destination. So when a keyword or key phrase emerges into conscious awareness, surrender to it — without second-guessing, censorship or judgment. Then let each succeeding word follow that one with the same freedom.

♪ ♪ ♪

Practice this brief meditation until you can do it anytime, anywhere: at home...in a restaurant or café...in a waiting room or departure lounge...on a walk...in a car, bus or subway...on a break at work...on a train or plane.

Allow at 10 to 20 minutes for this meditative exercise and for the writing experience that flows from it.

Go within, into your inner spiritual and emotional space, eyes open or closed as desired or required by your situation.

Breathe deeply. In and out five, ten or fifteen times to a count of five, six or seven.

Breathe in to your connection with your Muse or whatever you choose to call your creative source or creative spirit.

Breathe out all fears, anxieties, worries. Breathe out your immediate surroundings and all distractions they could inject into your awareness, into your space.

Breathe yourself into a place of creation and connection, a place where you are one with your words, your writing, your story, your project...your Muse.

After your fifth or tenth breath, or whenever it happens, reach within. Deep within. Reach within and let a word or phrase emerge.

Don't judge it. Don't actively choose it. Let it emerge. Writing on the Muse Stream is always about letting and allowing. Getting past your fears, blocks and resistance is also about letting and allowing. So let a word or phrase emerge from the depths of your being and allow it to bubble up to your conscious mind.

Allow yourself to hear it, to sense it, to know it. However you become aware of it is perfect, for you. Once you are aware of the word or phrase, let it flit and flitter down to your fingers, to your pen or keyboard. Let it flow onto the page or screen and allow yourself to flow from it. Without thinking. Without judging. Just being. Being that word, then the next, then the next.

As always on the Muse Stream, write without stopping — to think, judge, correct or edit. If you feel no words coming, use tools like repetition or free association or nonsense words to keep the flow alive. Or focus on your breath, writing "I am breathing in" as you inhale and "I am breathing out" as you exhale until the flow returns. It always does... if you let it.

So let it. And let the writing carry you on whatever journey of discovery your word or phrase sparks. The keyword or key phrase is your guide. Let it guide you, then, as you surrender to it and write.

After You've Written

The first thing most of us want to do after having written is to read our new creation. And our first impulse as we read it, especially if we have never written on the Muse Stream before, is to judge it. Harshly.

There are reasons for that.

When you write without thinking, without editing, without stopping, your language can be unrefined, your sentences can be incomplete and your emotions can be unfamiliar. The writer's voice you have known until this moment may not be present, usurped by something alien and disturbing. The thoughts and beliefs you have known until this moment may not be present, usurped by ones you could never imagine yourself holding.

What you write from the deep, heartful place to which your Muse Stream carries you can be raw...can seem strange...can be radically unlike anything you have ever written before.

It's natural to leap to judgment. That place of judgment serves neither you nor your work.

Chances are, judgment will prompt you to do one of two things: Abandon your work or hack at it mercilessly, homogenizing its prose and diluting its power.

Here is how to do it differently. After you've written, ask yourself these questions before looking at your work:

- Do I feel able to read my words from an openhearted place of non-judgment? Of objective discernment?
- Can I give myself permission to read it at least one time through without changing anything?
- Do I feel able to partner with my story rather than control it? To surrender to its wisdom?
- Can I give myself permission to read it from a place of respect and

compassion, for the work and for myself? From a place of trust in my innate creativity? In my Muse? In the essence of the work itself?

Unless you can answer yes, unequivocally, to all these questions, let your work sit unread until you can. Unless you can answer yes, you risk damaging your creation and your creativity by reading what you have written. Unless you can answer yes, it is premature to do anything with what you have written other than set it aside and write something else. It is certainly premature to edit or revise it.

When you can answer yes, pay special attention to "Rule" #8 in the next section, "12½ 'Rules' for Freeing Up Your Creative Flow." Pay close attention, as well, to the chapters on feedback in Section 10 ("Other Perspectives") before sharing your work with others.

How to edit your work is beyond the scope of this book. In brief, though, let your work sit quietly for a time before you launch into revision — be it a day, a week, a month or six months. The key is to give you and your work the space and distance that allow you to approach it heartfully, objectively and discerningly. That space and distance can vary from one piece of work to the next. It can even vary from one draft to the next. Respect your initial draft. Respect all your drafts. Don't be a slave to them. Allow your work to grow, change and mature. Allow yourself to grow, change and mature as its creator.

¶ *Practice compassion and non-judgment with these guided meditations: "Let Judgment Go" in Section 4 and "Making Friends with Your Inner Critic" in Section 8.*

¶ *Learn how to edit in a way that respects both your work and yourself as its creator in my book, "The Heartful Art of Revision: An Intuitive Guide to Editing."*

The Truth About Your Muse

In Greek mythology, the nine Muses were the daughters of gods Zeus and Mnemosyne. Goddesses in their own right, each Muse presided over an aspect of the arts and sciences — from history to hymns, comedy to poetry and astronomy to tragedy.

Today, whether or not personified by a woman, the Muse has come to symbolize creative inspiration for all artists. Or, as I put it in the "Meet Your Muse" meditation in the next chapter, your Muse is "the being that…embodies your purest creative source, that font of creative energy, inspiration and revelation that we all have within us."

Many writers view their Muse as a capricious adversary that makes itself available reluctantly and only when conditions are perfect. "My Muse has deserted me," writers complain. Or, "My Muse refuses to cooperate." Or, "My Muse is shy."

Those writers have it all wrong.

Muses are never shy. It is writers who are deaf or choose not to listen.

Muses are never uncooperative. It is writers who refuse to cooperate.

Muses never desert, hold back or resist. Writers desert, hold back and resist all the time.

In those moments when you believe your Muse is not working with you, ask yourself these questions…

- Where am I not surrendering unconditionally to my Muse and to the story it is calling on me to write?
- Which belief or way of life is my Muse challenging?
- What am I reluctant to face within myself that is holding me back from connecting with my Muse and writing my story?
- How is my resistance to change and inner growth preventing me from listening to my Muse and moving forward with my writing?
- Where else in my life or my creativity do I have resistance?

Exploration

Open your *Writer's Block Unblocked* journal and explore those questions as honestly as you dare, writing on the Muse Stream should you feel any resistance to accessing and expressing the truths of your heart. As you move forward with your writing from the answers, you will never again encounter a shy, uncooperative Muse.

Meet Your Muse

A Guided Meditation

Allow at least 30 minutes for this meditation and for the writing experience that flows from it.

My studio recording of this meditation is available for download or streaming as part "The Voice of the Muse Companion: Guided Meditations for Writers." See "Guided Meditations" in Section 1 ("Getting Started") to find out how to access the recording, as well as for tips on how best to use this book's meditations.

Relax. Close your eyes. Get into a comfortable position. Let your shoulders drop. And drop some more.

Take a few deep breaths, breathing in calm and quiet, breathing out fears, fatigue, stress. You're relaxed but alert. Awake and aware. Moving into a quiet place. A deep place. A place of creative freedom, creative vision, creative awakening.

In your mind's eye, see a door. A beautifully crafted door. Handcrafted. A work of art.

Perhaps it's a new door, newly discovered. Perhaps it's ancient, as old as time, waiting for you to rediscover it. See it or sense it...however you see it or sense it.

This is your doorway of inner vision. Walk up to it. Run your hand over it. Feel its texture...its richness...its depth.

As you touch the door, it swings open. The door to your inner vision will always swing open at your touch...if you let it.

You are the key.

Now the door swings open and you step across the threshold. Into a wondrous place.

Perhaps you recognize this place. Perhaps it's new to you.

Whatever you see or sense and however you see or sense it is perfect, perfect for you, in this moment.

See or sense this place, this wondrous place. See or sense it fully, using all your senses.

What does it look like? What colors do you see? How is the light? Do you hear any sounds? Smell any smells?

Reach out and touch something. Feel its texture.

What is the spirit of this place? What does it feel like, to you?

Now, coming toward you through this wondrous place, coming toward you bathed in light, is your Muse. Your creative spirit. The being that in this moment embodies your purest creative source, that font of creative energy, inspiration and revelation that we all have within us.

This is yours. Unique to you.

However it manifests, whatever you see, sense or feel of it, is right for you. In this moment.

Open your mind and heart. Allow it to come to you in whatever form it comes, recognizing that its form can change from moment to moment, mood to mood, writing project to writing project.

There is no right or wrong image, right or wrong way. There is only the way you see or sense, and what you see and sense. And it's perfect. For you.

What does your Muse look like? Feel like to you?

See or sense it fully. Again, use all your physical senses — sight, touch, smell, taste, sound. And your intuitive senses — feeling, spirit, essence.

Your Muse now stands before you, and you greet each other in whatever way feels right, taking all the time you need.

Now, you and your Muse begin a special dialogue.

Perhaps your Muse has a message for you. Perhaps you have questions for your Muse — questions about a specific project, questions about which is the right project for you right now, questions about your writing block, or general questions about your creative life.

Be open to whatever comes up. Let the dialogue go where it will.

Allow thirty seconds of silence for this conversation. Transcribe it if that will assist you. If you choose to write at this time, pause the meditation until you're done.

Now that you feel complete with that interaction, step forward. Take another step. Then another, moving closer and closer to your Muse... until you step into your Muse, until you and your Muse become one, merging in a wondrous moment of creative union.

What does that feel like? What sensations or emotions run through you? What do you see? Sense? Hear? Intuit?

Breathe deeply into the merged entity you are and experience all there is to experience...feel all there is to feel...be all there is to be.

Take twenty seconds of clock time to experience this fully.

Now that you feel complete, step back and away from your Muse. Note any feelings or sensations that action sparks for you. As you step away, thank your Muse for assisting you today and allow your Muse to respond.

Before you leave this place, your Muse hands you a gift, an expression of appreciation for having been freed into your life more consciously. What is it?

Receive this gift and keep it with you.

Recall it, if you choose, every time you sit down to write.

Now, turn back to the door — that special door — knowing that you can return to this place at any time to meet with your Muse. All you need to do is remember how it felt to be here. All it takes is stillness. A quiet time. A quiet place, where you're free to envision, where it's safe to create.

Once more, you touch the door, it swings open and you step through...and back.

As you return to your starting place, you bring back with you all you sensed and all you saw and all you heard, felt and intuited. You're bringing it back to your conscious awareness, remembering whatever, in this moment, it serves you to remember.

When you're ready, but only then, open your eyes, staying with all you experienced.

Write about it — what you saw, felt or sensed. Write about the conversation you had with your Muse. Write whatever you remember, whatever comes up, taking all the time you need.

Remember to keep your pen moving across the page. Remember to breathe. Remember to censor nothing, freeing the voice of your Muse to live again through you on the page.

4. 12½ "Rules" for Freeing Up Your Creative Flow

To be vulnerable is to live, to withdraw is to die.
JIDDU KRISHNAMURTI

Good writing is always about things that are important to you, things that are scary to you, things that eat you up.
JOHN EDGAR WIDEMAN

The "Rules"

These so-called rules aim to help free you from all that would hold you back in your creative life. And although the list continues to evolve — it's slightly different in each of my books for writers — the key rules never change.

The first and last are always designed to remind you that the only right way is the one that works for you today, and that nothing innovative or groundbreaking was ever conjured up by agreeing to be bound by someone else's rules or ways of doing things.

1. There Are No Rules
2. Get Out of Your Own Way
3. Leap into the Void...and Trust
4. Listen...and Always Go with First Thoughts
5. Surrender to the Muse Stream
6. Be In the Moment
7. Go for the Jugular
8. Love Yourself and Your Words
9. Strip Off Your Straitjackets
10. Write
11. Set Yourself Up for Success
12. Empower Yourself
12½. There Are No Rules

1. There Are No Rules

If you write anything based on rulebooks and the way things "should be," "must be" or "are supposed to be," you will produce work that is formulaic, manipulative and derivative. Moreover, you will be writing to today's tastes, trends and views, not to the ones that will be in effect when your work is finished and ready to be published or produced (see "The Market Is Fickle: Ignore Today's Trends" under "Rule" #9).

Yes, agents, editors, publishers, stage and film producers and competition judges set out submission requirements that you must adhere to if you want your work to be considered. These "rules," however, have nothing to do with either your creative flow or your story.

When it comes to your creative flow and your story, there are no fixed dictates, precepts, mandates or directives. How can there be when creativity is all about breaking new ground and breaking old rules? There is only *your* way...the way that works for you *today* (see "Rule" #6).

What about the rules of grammar, spelling and punctuation? Even those "rules" aren't really rules. There are infinite variations in what is considered acceptable — not only from one language and country to the next, but from one publishing house to the next. Ultimately, your top priority in that area will be consistency. Ultimately. Not now. That's because grammar, spelling and punctuation are *editing* concerns, not writing ones. They're especially irrelevant in your earliest drafts, when you're writing on the Muse Stream. So let those so-called rules go, too, until it's time to revise and edit your work.

I Did It My Way

I had no idea how to write a film script when a friend suggested I adapt my first novel, *The MoonQuest*, for the screen. That's why I dismissed the idea the first time she suggested it...and the second. The third and fourth too. Then one day it stuck.

Of course, I still didn't know how to write a screenplay, so I headed for the nearest bookstore. Traditional screenwriting methods, I knew, were highly structured; not my style at all. Could I find a handbook that was more intuitive? Could I also find one to help me adapt an existing work for the movies?

I couldn't. Everything on the shelf felt suffocatingly rule-bound. Even a string of online searches produced nothing helpful.

"You know all you need to know," the voice of my Muse insisted when I considered abandoning the project.

I was doubtful. My research made it clear that screenplays were technical, demanding creatures. Worse, there was apparently only one path to screenwriting success: the orthodox one. Detailed outlines (the more detailed the better) were mandatory. Index cards (to keep track of scenes) were compulsory. And an unwavering reverence for beats, plot points and three-act structure was obligatory. None of that was going to work for me.

Even if I could get past all the rules, where would I start? How would I start? And even if I found a way to start, then what? "I don't know all I need to know," I muttered. "I know nothing."

Then I recalled the opening pages of *The MoonQuest* and laughed. In that scene, Toshar knows he must tell his story but doesn't know where or how to begin. Then I remembered something else: Not knowing how to write a novel hadn't stopped me from starting *The MoonQuest* a decade earlier.

It wouldn't stop me from turning it into a screenplay now. I would do with *The MoonQuest* screenplay what I had done with the novel: I would break with convention and let the story guide me in its telling.

It did. The process wasn't effortless, and I was frequently plagued by judgment and self-doubt. But the screenplay got written...my way.

Then, because I had never found an intuitive guide to screenwriting, I wrote my own. The result? *Organic Screenwriting: Writing for Film, Naturally*. My first rule for screenwriting? You guessed it! "There are no rules."

Try This

Pull together some art supplies, call in your inner artist and create a large banner for your writing area that reads *Rule #1: There Are No Rules!* When your masterpiece is complete, post it somewhere that's always visible when you write. Also consider scanning it to use as the wallpaper on your computer and mobile devices.

EXPLORATION

Ask yourself these questions in your *Writer's Block Unblocked* journal but don't think about the answers. Let them emerge freely and honestly…on the Muse Stream, where appropriate. Let yourself be surprised by the answers.

- What "rules" do I feel bound by in my writing?
- How have they helped or hindered me?
- Which might I be ready to let go?

2. Get Out of Your Own Way

As you write — as part of an exercise, in your journal or on a directed project — the best way to stay connected with your Muse and the work at hand is to get out of your own way.

The writing experience need not be logical by any conventional or worldly standard, so ask any part of you that is logical, analytical, critical, cynical, doubt-filled or judgmental to step aside for the duration of your projected writing time.

By breathing into your heart and breathing out any fear, you will stay in the flow of inspiration and embark on a journey of infinite magic, wonder and awe.

Writing into Uncharted Territory

One of the questions I'm asked most often is, "Do you outline?" The short answer is no. Here's the longer answer...

An outline's gift and curse is that it provides you with a road map, which, in turn, sets out a destination for you to journey toward. Certainly, it's comforting and potentially more efficient to know where you're going.

Your outline, however, also carries risks: It can remove serendipity and surprise from the experience if you treat it as gospel and adhere to it unwaveringly, if you cling to it controllingly.

Some time ago, I had a Facebook discussion with a fellow writer about outlines. His argument went something like this: "The problem a lot of writers have is not being able to nail down exactly what their ending is before they start. That would be like getting in the car for a weekend getaway and not having any idea where you're going. Simply driving aimlessly, wasting a whole hell of a lot of gas. That's the value of a map, of an outline: If you know where you're going, you will get there, and usually in the most direct line."

It's ironic that my colleague used the "unmapped drive" example to criticize what he sees as the wastefulness of un-plotted writing. Going for a random, unplanned drive is the very example I have long used in my talks, workshops and coaching sessions to celebrate the magic of discovery, to illustrate what's involved in getting out of your own way. It's also the basis for the Muse Stream and for much of what I present in this and all my books for writers.

In my universe, it's more fun to get in the car, start it up and see where it will take me. Nearly always, it takes me somewhere I never could have imagined going, along a route I never would have thought of traveling. That unmapped drive is a near-perfect metaphor for how I write and how I live my life.

Can it be scary? Sometimes.

Can it feel out-of-control? Often.

Does it work? Always.

When I write, I sit in the passenger seat of the experience; I leave the steering wheel to the story. I do that because I view the story as its own sentient entity, one that knows its direction and imperative far better than I ever could. I know that if I let it take charge, it will introduce me to ideas, themes, characters and situations that my conscious mind would never have thought up...or permitted.

As for my life, had I determined a fixed destination and mapped out the quickest itinerary to reach it, I would have become neither a writer nor a parent, to name but two of the myriad, unexpected, amazing and transformative experiences I have lived over the past decades. I also would not be living in the United States as I write these words.

Like the greatest bulk of an iceberg, my deepest desires and greatest stories lie largely hidden in the ocean of my unconscious mind. The only way I know how to access them is through those leaps of faith that keep my controlling mind out of the process.

My directions in writing and life are neither energy-wasting nor aimless. Rather, they are guided by a wiser part of myself that knows both the destination and the way to reach it better than my conscious mind, as powerful and wonderful as it is, ever could. That's my map and GPS.

Do I outline? I never have. Even in high school when I was required to turn in an outline with my essays and term papers, I always wrote the paper first. I then crafted an outline to match it.

When I launch into a project, I rarely know the story in advance, let alone the ending. Although I had my screenplay for *The SunQuest* in front of me as I wrote the novel, I never prepared an outline for the screenplay. With my *Sara's Year* and *Emmeline Papers* novels, I thought I knew what the stories were about when the titles popped into my head. I was wrong in both cases. And in both cases, the stories that ultimately revealed themselves as I got out of my own way were infinitely better, more creative and more compelling than either original concept.

Even with *Writer's Block Unblocked*, where I had a title, a subtitle and a sense of my seven "solutions" before I began, I had no conscious idea how any of it would flesh out. I say no "conscious" idea, because the book itself knew what it was to be about. My job was to put it in the driver's seat so that I could sit back and enjoy the ride. Or, put another way, my job was to listen without judgment and to write without getting in the way of the book's superior wisdom.

How did I do that? By writing on the Muse Stream, by setting pen to paper or fingers to keyboard, allowing the river of words to flow on their own undirected course and trusting the voyage of discovery inherent in all creative life.

The story knows best. Always.

FEELING STUCK? TRY THIS...

Cultivate cliffhangers. What do I mean by that? If you're working on a project that involves multiple writing sessions over time and you aren't finding it easy to get back to it from one session to the next, suspend your day's writing in the middle of a scene or thought or even of a sentence. When you pick up the next day, you won't be starting with a blank page. Instead, you will already know what you need to write next.

Alternatively, use the final sentence of whatever you wrote last as the key phrase for the day's writing. Perhaps it will be a continuation (that's how I wrote the first draft of *The MoonQuest*); perhaps it will be the start of something new. Get out of your own way, surrender to the journey and see where it takes you.

3. Leap into the Void...and Trust

Trust that every word you are ready to write exists in the inkwell of your pen or somewhere deep in the inner workings of your computer or mobile device.

Follow that pen wherever it takes you. Don't push it across the page. Surrender to it. Don't force down the keys of your keyboard; let those keys engage of their own accord and let your fingers follow along with them.

Trust the voice of your Muse without judgment or censorship. Don't worry about being polite, appropriate or correct. Don't worry about making sense. Don't worry about anything. Just blurt it out. What seems silly in the moment is nearly always higher truth...or art.

Your Story Is Smarter Than You Are

You may think that this story you are writing (or not writing) was your idea. It's probably more accurate to suggest that you were the story's idea. After all, it was the story that summoned you to convert its formless energy into form...into words on a page. So discard all notions that you're in charge and give up all pretense at control. You're not the boss. Your story is.

Why let your story be in charge? Because it's smarter than you are. Because it knows what it's about better than you ever will. Because you are writing *its* story, not yours.

Given that, you might as well forget *everything* you think you know about it. Instead, approach your story with an open heart and an open mind. Don't force your will onto it. Talk to it. Sit in the silence with it. Listen to it. Follow its lead. Let it have its way with you. If you do, it will write itself for you.

Exploration

Ask yourself these questions in your *Writer's Block Unblocked* journal but don't think about the answers. And don't feel you have to answer each question independently if that doesn't feel right.

Let your individual answers (or whatever single answer these questions trigger) emerge freely and honestly, writing them on the Muse Stream in a free-flowing, stream-of-consciousness way where appropriate. Let yourself be surprised by the answers.

- Where have I been resisting my story's superior wisdom?
- Where in my relationship with my story and my Muse can I be more openhearted and surrendered?
- In what other ways can I trust my story? Can I let it be boss?

Toss Out the Itinerary

Years ago, before there were smartphones or an internet, I booked a trip to Europe, knowing nothing but my initial destination and the date and airport of my final departure. I traveled light, with no checked bags, and I had nothing to guide me, apart from a Eurailpass, a few guidebooks and the maps and train schedules I picked up along the way.

For six weeks I wandered from city to city and country to country, following my intuition and the voice of my heart — even though at the time I had no conscious awareness of either. It was a trip much like the ones I describe in "Writing into Uncharted Territory," filled with the unexpected encounters, amazing discoveries and extraordinary experiences that always show up for us when we abandon control and embrace the mystery.

Exploration 1

Have you ever started your car and taken off with no clear itinerary and no fixed destination? Have you ever gone for an aimless walk, just to see where your feet would carry you? Have you ever boarded a bus, subway or commuter train with no plan other than to enjoy the ride, wherever it takes you? Now is the time to try any or all of those experiences.

Turn off your cellphone and take off. Walk, drive, take public transit or mix 'n match your modes of transport. Give yourself a full morning or afternoon or, if you can spare it, a full day. Stop somewhere you've never been for coffee or a meal. Strike up a conversation with a stranger. Pop into a store or a park or a museum or some other site of conventional or unconventional interest along the way, preferably a place you're visiting for the first time. And do your best to not return along the same route.

When you get back, write about your experiences in your *Writer's Block Unblocked* journal. Where did you go? What did you see? What did you discover? What was fun? What was less fun? Who did you talk to and what did you talk about? Then, continuing in your journal, explore what it would feel like if you gave yourself permission to do more of that in your writing life.

Exploration 11

Surrender to *your* journey. Open your mind to those parts of your story you have not allowed yourself to see — both on your page and in your life. Allow yourself to experiment with new forms, new genres, new paper, new pens. Venture out onto the ledge of your consciousness and creativity and take the leap that will transform the world — beginning with your own.

4. Listen...and Always Go with First Thoughts

Just start, and trust your story and its characters (if you're writing fiction) to propel you into worlds beyond your conscious imagining.

Write the first thing that comes into your head — whatever it is. Second thoughts and second-guessing arise from that part of your mind that is judgmental or censoring. First thoughts carry you past your fear and resistance to the heart of your story.

Trust that what is coming to you is what calls out to be expressed. Allow it to be expressed, unconditionally.

The Wisdom of First Thoughts

First thoughts often guide our stories along meandering paths and in baffling directions, their wisdom rarely making itself apparent until chapters later. When I was writing the first draft of *The MoonQuest*, for example, those first thoughts would regularly push the story in ways that initially made no sense to me. I was nearly always tempted to rein in the plot, to force the story to go where I believed it ought to go instead of where it seemed to want to go.

When I surrendered to the story and went with first thoughts instead of second-guessing it, instead of imposing my will on it, what emerged was always more engaging, more compelling, more creative and truer to its themes and characters than anything my conscious mind could have conjured up.

Sometimes, the wisdom of those first thoughts doesn't make itself known until several books later. It wasn't until I wrote *The SunQuest* and *The Bard of Bryn Doon* that certain of *The MoonQuest*'s events, plot twists and character attributes finally made sense. Had I second-guessed and blocked those *MoonQuest* first thoughts, later books in the series would have suffered.

The story of my life has been no different…is no different. As I do with my writing, I let the meandering paths and baffling directions of the chapters I'm living carry me where they will. Even in those moments when those paths and directions make no sense, I do my best to ignore my mind's attempt at second-guessing and trust the wisdom of the story.

Exploration

Ask yourself these questions in your *Writer's Block Unblocked* journal but don't think about the answers. And don't feel you have to answer each question independently if that doesn't feel right.

Let your individual answers (or whatever single answer these questions trigger) emerge freely and honestly, writing them on the Muse Stream in a free-flowing, stream-of-consciousness way where appropriate. Let yourself be surprised by the answers.

- Where in my writing have I second-guessed, censored and/or blocked my first thoughts?
- How might my writing have been different had I trusted those first thoughts?
- How can I now be more open to the voice of my Muse, which always speaks in first thoughts?
- Where in my *life* have I second-guessed, censored and/or blocked my first thoughts? How might my life have been different had I trusted those first thoughts? Moving forward, how might my life be different if I let myself trust them more?

5. Surrender to the Muse Stream

Free your pen to keep flowing across the page or your fingers to keep dancing across the keyboard. Don't stop for any reason. Make up words if you must, but keep writing. If you feel you can't, if nothing comes, revisit "Seven Surefire Ways to Navigate the Muse Stream," (Section 2).

Writing into the Chaos

When I began *The MoonQuest*, I wasn't certain that the Muse Stream philosophy I was already teaching would work for a full-length work. To my amazement, it did. I wrote the first draft, all four hundred pages or so, on the Muse Stream. And it *was* chaotic. There were no chapter breaks; names, places and descriptions changed from one part of the manuscript to the next; and repetition was rampant. Yet, as I listened, trusted and surrendered (not without resistance), the chaos sorted itself out.

Can you trust your story, whatever it is, enough to let it guide you? Can you trust your Muse enough to let go fully, knowing that it will guide you equally well through future drafts — all the way to your final draft?

Whatever your next project is, write your first draft in nonstop free-flow on the Muse Stream, as you are doing with this book's exercises. Write, allowing your first draft to be as messy, chaotic and disordered as it needs to be...as you need it to be. And discover the magic and hidden treasures that only reveal themselves when you leap into the void...and trust.

If the Muse Stream Is Good Enough for Francis Ford Coppola, It's Good Enough for You!

The Muse Stream, as I will continue to remind you, is about writing without stopping. Not stopping to correct spelling, punctuation or grammar. Not stopping to edit. Not stopping to grope for the right word. Not stopping to worry whether what you've written is good enough. The Muse Stream is about always moving forward — to the next word, to the next page, to the next chapter.

What does this have to do with Francis Ford Coppola? When the Oscar-winning writer-director (*The Godfather*, among others) works on a screenplay, he never looks back over what he has already written, and he never rewrites until he is ready to start his next draft.

"You have a lot of doubts when you read in unfinished fragments," Coppola told *Creative Screenwriting* magazine in 2009. "There's almost a hormone that secretes from writers to hate what they're writing, so you get fooled into reworking and changing it."

Surrendering to the Muse Stream, as I wrote here earlier, means going with first thoughts, committing to the page whatever leaps first into your mind, however wacky it might seem. In fact, the wackier it feels, the more likely it is that your inner censor is interfering with your creative process.

"Wacky" is a judgment. It comes from that fearful, second-thoughts, second-guessing part of you that is trying to protect you from straying into dangerous territory, that is afraid you will be judged harshly for what you are about to write.

Going with first thoughts helps you bypass that inner critic and get your most creative thoughts onto the page before those logical, analytical, critical, cynical, doubt-filled or judgmental parts of you can stop them.

"It's counterproductive," Coppola noted in that same article, "to start judging it before you've allowed the whole trip to take place."

That's the creative reason for surrendering to the Muse Stream. There is also a practical reason.

What if you start your story and, before moving forward to your second chapter or scene, you spend days and weeks polishing, perfecting and otherwise tweaking your first-draft opening?

Nothing wrong with that, right?

Wrong.

Here's why. What if, when you begin your second draft, you realize that your opening is not as brilliant as you had originally thought? What if, as you reread those weeks of work, you realize that not only is it not brilliant, it's not even salvageable?

As you hold down the delete key over all that work, you'll be thinking of all the time you wasted. Wouldn't your time have been better spent surrendering to the Muse Stream? Wouldn't you have made more progress had you written without going back to rewrite, had you kept moving forward?

There's a time and place for revision and rewriting; it's not while you are in your Muse Stream's creative flow. And as I point out in *The Heartful Art of Revision: An Intuitive Guide to Editing*, revision need not be the slash-and-burn, left-brain assault you might have been taught. It can be as intuitive as your acts of creation — and as effective.

EXPLORATION

Ask yourself these questions in your *Writer's Block Unblocked* journal but don't think about the answers. And don't feel you have to answer each question independently if that doesn't feel right.

Let your individual answers (or whatever single answer these questions trigger) emerge freely and honestly, writing them on the Muse Stream in a free-flowing, stream-of-consciousness way where appropriate. Let yourself be surprised by the answers.

- Do I stop to edit as I write?
- Do I stop to think about what to write next?
- Do I stop to think about how people will react to what I'm writing?
- Am I looking backward instead of continuing to move forward with my story?
- Am I letting my doubts and judgments get in the way of the natural free-flow of my creativity? (If you are, "Rule" #8 is for you.)

- Are there other ways in which I consistently resist the Muse Stream?

If you answered yes to any of those questions, redouble your efforts, *without beating yourself up*, to follow the Muse Stream's basic precepts as you write. Modify them to meet the needs of your story, but don't dilute them.

Relax. It's Only Your First Draft...

First drafts are messy. First drafts are chaotic. First drafts are disordered. First drafts are inconsistent. First drafts are meandering. First drafts are repetitive. First drafts are too long, or too short. That's why they are *first* drafts.

First drafts are journeys of discovery. In your first draft, you leap into the void to find out what your story is and what it's about. If you are writing fiction, you learn who your characters are. Fiction or nonfiction, you encounter ideas, beliefs and convictions you never knew you had. Fiction or nonfiction, you come face-to-face with shadow selves that, more than likely, have long resided hidden within you.

Your first draft is that unplanned drive into the country, that map-free journey filled with synchronicities, serendipities and surprises. Your first draft is where you taste the magic of the written word and experience the alchemy of creation. Your first draft is where you let the story and its characters reveal to you what and who they are, which may resemble nothing that you expected. Your first draft is your first experience of surrender, where you begin to discover that you don't own the story, where you begin to discover that the story owns you.

Don't go into your first draft expecting it to be your final draft. Neither draft will ever be perfect, but your first probably won't even be excellent. It might not even be good. It might, in fact, be really, really, terrible. Let it be that. Let it be what it is: an exploration...a journey...a voyage into the unknown. Let it be your leap of faith into the void, your act of surrender to your Muse. And let it, along with every draft up to your final draft, be the perfectly imperfect expression of a transcendent vision that is uniquely yours.

Still Feeling Stuck? Try This...

Tell the story you're seeking to tell without worrying about form, structure, flow or facts. Ignore punctuation. Forget complete sentences if that helps. Or jot down whatever random thoughts come to you, regardless of their order or relevance.

If you're writing fiction, focus only on dialogue or forgo dialogue altogether in favor of straight narrative. If you're writing nonfiction, make the points you're seeking to make without the need to prove or justify them.

If you're working on a screenplay, it's easy to get bogged down — or stopped — by screenwriting's rigid format requirements. When that happens, leave screenplay format behind and continue your storytelling as an unformatted prose narrative. Convert the scene or scenes back into script form once you have regained the thread of your story or at the start of your next writing session. Or leave it until your next draft.

6. Be In the Moment

Be in the moment with each word...word by word. The word that trips off your fingers and onto the page or keyboard is the only one that matters. Were you to stop and think about each word, were you to stop to analyze, judge and left-brain each word, there would be no next word. So stay in the flow. Remember, the next word always comes...if you don't worry about it. If you let it.

One Step at a Time...One Word at a Time

There's a scene in *The MoonQuest* where Toshar, the main character, steps onto a translucent road, his sole route back to earth from a celestial plateau high above the suns (there are two suns in the world of the book).

"I quickly learned," Toshar recounts in the story, "to train my eyes to look no more than a few paces ahead. At that distance, a faint, silvery glow marked out my path. It was almost opaque. Yet if I looked back or farther ahead, I saw no sign of road. No sign of anything." In Toshar's world, as in yours and mine, the past and future have no substance. Only the present moment exists...the present moment and the present word. Don't look back and don't worry forward. As you write, stay in the moment, word-by-word.

Ironically, that's the same journey I traveled in writing *The MoonQuest*, a book whose story I knew nothing about except as I wrote it. The novelist E.L. Doctorow has likened writing to driving at night in the fog. "You can only see as far as your headlights," he wrote, "but you can make the whole trip that way." Some days on *The MoonQuest*, Doctorow's headlights showed me the next scene. Some days, they showed me only the next sentence. Some days, only the next word. Yet as I surrendered to the journey — and to the voice of my Muse — the story unfolded, magnificently, and in ways I could never have predicted, plotted or envisioned. I have had similar experiences with all my books, nonfiction as well as fiction.

As we move forward, writing the word or sentence of the moment, the next will always appear...if we are open to it. If we have our eyes on the road and our headlights on, if we are prepared to trust in the unknown that lies just beyond the reach of our vision, that unknown will become illuminated, known and manifest.

Try This

In today's writing, notice all the times your mind edges (or leaps) ahead of the word you're writing. Be aware as that controlling part of yourself reaches forward to find out what's coming next, where you're headed, how it will end. Notice when this happens, but don't judge or punish yourself. Instead, return your focus to the word of the moment. Return to it gently, lovingly, reassuringly. And continue writing, in the moment, letter by letter and word by word.

Try This Too

Go for a walk — in nature, around the block, down a busy street or anywhere that offers you some degree of sensory stimulation. As you walk, do your best to stay in the present moment, focusing only on your five senses and on what you are seeing, hearing, touching, smelling or tasting from breath to breath. If you find your mind wandering, make a point of acknowledging each stimulus, saying (aloud or silently), "I see/smell/hear/touch/taste the..." Repeat the phrase as you walk, as often as necessary to keep focused on the now. By staying in the moment, we stay out of fear, worry and anxiety, prime causes of all blocks — in our lives as much as in our writing.

Try This As Well

Write on the Muse Stream using the key phrase "In this moment, I am..." as your kickoff. Don't think about what to write. Don't censor or second-guess what emerges. Free onto the page the words, thoughts and feelings that want to emerge and let them reveal to you where you truly are in this moment. After you have written for a few minutes, begin again using the same key phrase: "In this moment, I am..." Later, write on the Muse Stream from any of these mini-vignettes and see where it takes you. As a variation on this exercise, use the phrase "In this moment, I write about..."

EXPLORATION

Ask yourself this question in your *Writer's Block Unblocked* journal but don't think about the answer. Let it emerge freely and honestly on the Muse Stream.

- Where in my creative and life's journey can I more fully trust that the headlights illuminating my way will carry me to my unseen destination?

Grounded in the Moment
A GUIDED MEDITATION

Use this brief meditation to return your focus to the present moment any time you find your mind wandering.

Allow 10 to 15 minutes for this experience.

Sit down — at your desk, in your favorite chair, in your favorite part of the garden, in your favorite park or on your favorite beach...wherever you feel comfortable, safe and inspired. Or lie down. Do whatever is easiest and most convenient.

Close your eyes, place your hands on your empty lap, or on your abdomen if you're lying down, and breathe...in and out slowly, as slowly as you can, for ten breaths.

Breathe more slowly and deeply with each breath, and feel yourself relax. Feel each inhalation connect you to your heart, to the moment and to whatever higher power you believe in.

Feel each exhalation flush all fear, doubt and anxiety from your emotional body...flush all worldly concerns from your mind.

As you continue to breathe in and out, let your breath dissolve all tightness from your physical body — from your neck and shoulders, from your chest and abdomen, from your mid- and lower back and from any other place where you cling to stress and tension.

Now, as your breath continues to slow and deepen, focus on your heart and breathe into it and into the only moment that exists: that place of the eternal now.

Now, I would like you to picture yourself in a park or on a beach, holding on to a bunch of brightly colored balloons, each with its own string. There's a slight breeze in the air, and the balloons are bobbing around and bouncing into each other.

As you continue to relax and breathe, you may notice your mind straying from the present moment with a thought about the past or future. Perhaps you are replaying a moment from earlier in your day or from years back. Or perhaps you are thinking ahead — to a bill that needs paying...to an upcoming appointment...or to anything that is not of this moment, that is not of this breath.

Whatever your not-now thought, assign it to one of the balloons. To any balloon. Let a short version of your thought inscribe itself onto the surface of that balloon and, once it has, I would like you to release that balloon. Let it go and let it float up into the air. Watch it rise higher and higher in the sky, and be aware of it growing smaller and smaller until, finally, it disappears into the distance. As it vanishes from view, let the thought you attached to it vanish as well.

Continue releasing those thought-balloons one-by-one until you are able to stay present in the moment with your breath, then rest in the stillness of the eternal now until you feel complete with the experience.

When you do feel complete, slowly bring your awareness back to your physical body and to your surroundings.

Become conscious of your arms and legs, of your hands and feet, of your neck and shoulders. Move or shake them gently. Become aware again of your breath, of your heartbeat.

Notice any ambient sounds — in the room or beyond. What are you hearing? Sensing around you?

Now, become aware of whatever you are sitting or lying on. Let your fingers run over it and feel its texture, its temperature, its solidity, its hardness or softness.

When you're ready, let your eyes open and adjust to the light. Sit up if you're lying down. Connect once again with the physicality and energy of your surroundings.

Finally, and only when you feel it's time, allow yourself to reenter the world, whatever that means to you, from a place of the same moment-to-moment awareness you experienced in the meditation.

In the hours and days ahead, use this thought-balloon imagery to release anything that is pulling you from the present moment or away from the words you are writing.

Variation: If the balloon image doesn't work for you, or if you want to try something different, imagine yourself in a room holding a broom. Each time you find yourself pulled out of the present moment, open the door and sweep that thought away.

7. Go for the Jugular

Go for *your* jugular. Let yourself be vulnerable. Go for the demon you would run from. Go for the feeling you would flee from. Go for the emotion you would deny. Go for the memory you would repress. Once you put it on paper, you strip it of its power over you. Once you put it on paper, you free it to empower your work.

"Walk the Earth Naked, Clothed Only in Your Truth"

On the morning of my forty-second birthday, I packed my few belongings into my Dodge Caravan and, for the fifth time in two years, followed my heart along the asphalt road of my soul's journey. My destination? A two-room flat in the rural outskirts of Penetanguishene, a summer-resort town a hundred miles north of Toronto on the shores of Lake Huron.

Why was I there? If I needed a reason to satisfy my logical mind, it was to write a new draft of *The MoonQuest*. I would soon discover deeper reasons.

My fifth night in my new home, I awoke from a violent nightmare with the phrase "I just want to say something" echoing in my consciousness. That line, so emblematic of the longstanding blocks to my self-expression that *The MoonQuest* was helping to dissolve, haunted me until I wrote it down. What emerged from those six words was an "inner dialogue"[1] of such transformative depth that I knew I had to keep at it.

I had often turned to inner or meditative dialogue to deepen my

---

[1] See Exploration I at the end of this chapter to learn how to have your own inner or meditative dialogue.

journaling. But never before had the words cascaded out of me so passionately and, in the ensuing weeks, so frequently.

Although I had not yet heard of Neale Donald Walsch's still-new *Conversations with God*, my writings — which quickly titled themselves *Dialogues with the Divine* — were taking on a similar form and tone. Reluctant to expose my uncomfortably raw emotions to the world, I resisted viewing them as part of any sort of manuscript. But the same "Divine" voice that came through on the page so reassuringly had its forceful side. If it didn't immediately demand that I turn these conversations into a book, it did insist that I stop hiding — from myself.

As a frozen Ontario winter began to thaw into spring, I unmasked one demon after another. All found their uncensored way onto the page, ultimately distilled into their single essence: Fear. Fear of judgment. Fear of my vision. Fear of my voice. Fear of my power. Fear of the emptiness from which all creation emerges. Fear of the unmasking process itself.

My greatest fear, of course, was not about shedding my masks while standing in front of a mirror. It was about removing those masks before stepping out the front door. Self-awareness was terrific. I was all for it. But exposing all those perceived flaws to the world? That left me too vulnerable. That was too dangerous.

"I feel naked," I wrote one day. "I feel exposed. People will laugh. People will judge. People will destroy me, annihilate me. It's too much."

The words that emerged in response were even more terrifying: "Walk the earth naked, clothed only in your truth. Book or no book is not the issue. Coming out is the issue. Being out in the world with your truth is the issue."

This was not about coming out as a gay man. I had done that more than a decade earlier with minimal fallout. It was about coming out as frightened, vulnerable and imperfect. It was about coming out as human.

One evening I printed out three freshly written scenes from *The MoonQuest* and took them with me to The Daily Perk, a café in nearby Midland. It was Thursday, open-mic night, and I was determined to walk the earth in one of the most naked ways a writer can: by reading from his work-in-progress to a live audience.

These were not ordinary scenes. They were scenes of nightmarish horror like none I had ever written, scenes that revealed a dark, violent part of me that I was reluctant to acknowledge, let alone share with a room full of strangers.

These were scenes that made me uncomfortable, that embarrassed me, that made me feel dangerously vulnerable. They were also scenes that I spent the next decade trying to justify excising from the manuscript.

It wasn't until the published book had been out a year that I understood why they were so integral to the story. Actually, I had to be told why — by a facilitator who was teaching a class based on *The MoonQuest* at Unity Santa Fe, which, ironically, nearly banned the book from its bookstore because of those controversial scenes.

"*The MoonQuest* is about the power of storytelling," the facilitator explained. "It's a story about what is destroyed when we're prevented from telling our stories and about the healing that occurs when we break through the silence and share those stories with each other."

Put another way, it's about the power of vulnerability.

∫   ∫   ∫

It would take seventeen years for *Dialogues with the Divine*, by then subtitled *Encounters with My Wisest Self*, to "walk the world" as a published book, finally revealing the pain and perceived failings I alone had come to know during my five-month sojourn in Penetanguishene. But the call for me to walk the earth naked, clothed only in my truth would repeat itself again and again in the intervening years.

It repeats itself in every book, whose teachings I live and relive, not always comfortably, in the writing of them. It will continue to repeat itself as I live and write more and more openly in the days, months and years ahead. For only when I allow myself to be vulnerable, only when I walk the earth naked clothed only in my truth, am I living — and writing — my truest, most authentic self.

Exploration 1

To experience your own inner dialogue, get into a meditative state, ask a question that's important to you and allow the answer to emerge on the Muse Stream. Once you have your answer, continue the "conversation" until you feel complete.

Writing fiction? Adapt this technique to engage in dialogue with your characters. You'll be amazed by what you discover about them and about your story.

Exploration 11

Ask yourself these questions in your *Writer's Block Unblocked* journal but don't think about the answers. And don't feel you have to answer each question independently if that doesn't feel right.

Let your individual answers (or whatever single answer these questions trigger) emerge freely and honestly, writing them on the Muse Stream in a free-flowing, stream-of-consciousness way where appropriate. Let yourself be surprised by the answers.

- Where in my writing am I refusing to reveal myself to others? Why?
- Where in my writing am I refusing to reveal myself to me? How? Why?
- Where in my writing am I holding back from experiencing and sharing powerful emotions, especially those I would prefer to avoid?
- Where in my writing am I refusing to be vulnerable and authentic? To be human? What is holding me back?
- Where in my writing am I stopping myself from walking the earth naked, clothed only in my truth?
- Where in my writing, directly or indirectly, can I begin to share my pain and passion? My dreams and desires? My missteps and mistakes? My imperfection? My joy?
- Where in my writing can I come out of hiding? Where can I be less self-conscious? Be more authentic? Be more vulnerable?

¶ See also "12½ 'Rules' for Living a Creative Life" in Section 13.

The Mask

A Guided Meditation

Allow at least 30 minutes for this experience and for the writing that flows from it.

Close your eyes. Let your hands fall to your lap if you're sitting, to your abdomen if you're lying down.

Breathe...deeply...in and out...in and out...in and out...letting your breath slow and deepen with each inhalation, with each exhalation.

As you breathe in and out, feel your jaw loosen...your shoulders drop...your whole body relax. Feel relaxation course through your body. Feel it carried by your bloodstream. Feel your bloodstream as a river of calm, relaxation, love and empowerment. Of safety.

Know that at any time during this experience, if anything feels too dangerous, all you have to do is take a deep breath and open your eyes. All you have to do is suspend this meditative journey until you feel able to continue. You are safe. You are safe.

Continue to breathe, to breathe deeply into this experience...into this journey into the heart of you. Focus on your breath, and as you inhale and exhale, I am going to ask you a series of questions. Either answer them in your mind within this meditative experience or pause the meditation while you open your eyes and journal your answers. Whichever works for you. There is no right or wrong way of doing it, just as there is no right or wrong answer to any of these questions.

So...my questions...

- What in your life and/or writing are you self-conscious about?
- What about yourself or your writing do you fear? Do you refuse to experience or express out in the world?

Don't think too hard about this. Simply let a few responses bubble up into your conscious awareness — without judgment and without censorship. Allow yourself to open. Allow yourself to be surprised.

Are you surprised?

Now, go deeper. Look into more places in your life and creative life where you are self-conscious. Peer into the dark closets of your reluctance, the dust-filled attics of your concealment, the clammy cellars of your fear.

- Where are you embarrassed? Ashamed?
- Where do you feel inadequate?
- Where are you afraid of being judged?
- Where are you holding yourself back?
- Where are you hiding?
- Where are you not willing to risk being seen?

Each of those places is a mask you wear out into the world. Perhaps it's a mask you wear in front of the mirror. Regardless, it is a mask. And like all masks, it separates you not only from the rest of the world, but from yourself.

I'd like you focus on one of those masks right now. Only one. Any one. Can you get a sense of what it looks like? You might not experience this visually, and that's okay. There is no right or wrong way to experience any part of this meditation.

Whether or not you can see the mask, what does it feel like? What does it feel like on your face? What does it feel like in your heart? More importantly, perhaps, what is that mask holding you back from feeling? More important still: What is it holding you back from experiencing? From expressing? From writing? From being? From becoming?

Journal your answers if that feels right. Or simply let them bubble to the surface of your conscious mind. Either way, sit with them for a few minutes. Let them sit with you.

Do you know why you created that mask? Do you have a story that explains it? That justifies it? Of course, you do. We all have good and powerful reasons for the masks we wear. Or, more accurately, we *had* good reasons for creating those masks...once upon a time.

But that time is not this time. That time was then, when we needed their protection. This time is now, when we are stronger, braver and more aware than ever that our masks are not ours alone. They are everyone's. And because they are everyone's, they not only hold us back, they hold everyone back.

So, whatever your reason for donning that mask, however long ago you slipped it on, that reason no longer exists, at least not in the same way it did in that "once upon a time." Can you acknowledge that? And in acknowledging that, can you also acknowledge that that mask no longer serves you in the ways it was originally designed? And in acknowledging that, can you also acknowledge that it is holding back your writing — holding *you* back — in some way? Some significant way?

And from that acknowledgment, can you consider lifting that mask from your face? Can you accept that it's okay to show your face, to be yourself? To be yourself first to yourself? Can you accept that it's okay to come out of hiding? To let yourself be seen? To let yourself be vulnerable?

Take a deep breath. As deep as you can. Breathe in all the strength of the universe. Breathe in all the courage of the universe. Breathe in all the love of the universe.

Now, touch your hand to your face. To the mask. And as you do and as you breathe, fully and deeply, let the mask dissolve at your touch. Let it dissolve and reveal the beauty and light that you are. Let it reveal the divine perfection that you are. Let it reveal the humanity that you are.

Be with that unmasked face for a few moments. How does it feel? It's okay to feel scared, if you do. It's natural to feel scared, to feel raw, to feel vulnerable. All that means is that you're feeling human. That's because feeling, whatever it is you feel, is what it means to be human.

It's also natural to feel lighter, freer, more open to possibility and the fullest expression of your potential — on the page and in your life.

Feel whatever you feel. Breathe into that feeling. Be okay with that feeling. Sit with that feeling for a few moments. Take some time to let that feeling evolve.

If this is not your first experience with this meditation and you feel able to dissolve another mask, go ahead and do it.

If this is your first experience, be gentle with yourself. Give yourself time to fully integrate and embody what it feels like to have let go this one mask. You can always return tomorrow or next week to remove another.

Regardless, take all the time you now need to remain in this meditative space before becoming once more fully aware of your breath, your physical body and your surroundings as a prelude to stepping back into your everyday life, now lighter, freer and more authentically you.

¶ *See also "Say No to Shame" under Surefire Solution #1, Section 8.*

8. Love Yourself and Your Words

Treat your creation as an act of the heart. Love whatever issues from your pen without judgment. Every word. Every paragraph. Every draft. Be gentle with yourself.

¶ *If you can't help but judge, revisit "After You've Written" (Section 3) before reading over any of your writing.*

¶ *See "Other Perspectives" (Section 10) and "On Rejection" (Section 11) for tips on when and how to seek feedback on your work and on what to do when you're criticized harshly or rejected.*

Say "No" to Judgment

How often have you judged yourself or your words harshly? How often, in a first, subsequent or final draft, have you cried out, "This isn't good enough." Or, "This will never be good enough." Or, "This story has been told better by someone else." Or, "This book, short story, poem, song, essay, stage play or screenplay has been written before." Or, "My opinion, outlook, perspective or philosophy isn't original, valid, well-presented or well-written."

What you have written *is* good enough…in this moment. Does that mean you can't improve it in the next moment? Of course it doesn't. That's what revisions are for. In this moment, however, your words and work deserve to be celebrated as an integral step on your creative path, one no less valid and valuable than any other.

Remember: If you do your best to write freely and easily from your heart, what emerges onto the page is always good enough. It is always better than good enough. It is as close to perfection as is possible.

One more thing: It doesn't matter if others have written their own version of your story. What matters in this moment is *your* version. How many riffs exist on the Romeo and Juliet story? How many retellings have there been of the Greek myths? How many times have you been entertained by a fresh take on the boy-meets-girl/boy-loses-girl/boy-finds-girl formula that is the staple of romantic comedy?

Whatever your story is, no one can tell it the way you can. No one has your unique perspective. No one has had your particular set of experiences. No one can weave a tale the way you can. Be true to your heart, your Muse and your story, and no one else's version will matter.

Write what you must in the way only you can. Trust the superior wisdom of your story. And give yourself permission to write the worst junk in the world, knowing that you have all the time in the world to hone and shape it into excellence.

EXPLORATION

Ask yourself these questions in your *Writer's Block Unblocked* journal but don't think about the answers. And don't feel you have to answer each question independently if that doesn't feel right.

Let your individual answers (or whatever single answer these questions trigger) emerge freely and honestly, writing them on the Muse Stream in a free-flowing, stream-of-consciousness way where appropriate. Let yourself be surprised by the answers.

- Can I give myself permission to write junk?
- Can I honor each stage in my creative life and trust that my work will improve — from draft to draft and from project to project?
- In what other ways do I judge and/or criticize myself and/or my writing? In what ways have those negative judgments played out in my writing? In my life? Held me back?
- In what ways have I beat myself up this week? Today? (Be honest!) How can I make amends? What one act of self-love can I commit to right now?

Close your eyes for a moment. Focus on your breath. Be present. With your words. With your writing. In your life.

Let Judgment Go...and Let Your Story Flow
A Guided Meditation

Allow at least 30 minutes to complete this meditation and for the writing that flows from it.

My studio recording of this meditation is available for download or streaming as part "The Voice of the Muse Companion: Guided Meditations for Writers." See "Guided Meditations" in Section 1 ("Getting Started") to find out how to access the recording, as well as for tips on how best to use this book's meditations.

Breathe. Breathe in the quiet, white light of your creative essence, your divine essence, your Muse. Breathe in your fire, your flame, your beingness, your God-self. Breathe in the light of who you are, the truth of who you are, the love of who you are.

Breathe in all the light and aloha you are.

Aloha is not merely a word that conjures up the gentle swaying of palm trees and hula dancers. Aloha is a consciousness, a state of being, a state of openheartedness, a state of love in its truest, fullest sense.

Breathe into that openness within you. Breathe it in fully, deeply, completely.

Breathe out any doubts, any fears that you're not good enough, that someone else or anyone else — your friend who has already been published, your neighbor who writes better description than you do — is a more accomplished creator.

Breathe that out, for it is not true.

You are creative. You are innately creative. You are inherently creative. Everyone is. And because you are, you can express that creativity through writing, through placing one word after the next on the written page.

Let go of all feelings that you're not good enough. For you are. Release all feelings that others are better than you. They are not. You are equal to all and equal to the joyful task at hand, which is expressing the words and passions of your heart in written form. You are equal to it, for you were born to it. Every micro-bit, every nano-bit of your being — physical, emotional and spiritual — has been encoded with that will, desire and aptitude to create.

You may lack certain skills. Those skills can be learned and practiced. In this moment, skills don't matter nearly as much as heart, intent and choice. You have the former. We all do. And you can tap into the latter two with ease.

Know that and be that.

It's simple. It's simple yet complex, for you are pushing against what may seem like lifetimes of programming.

What has been programmed can be erased — more quickly than the time it took to program into you.

You are good enough. You are better than good enough.

Despite what anyone ever said, despite any way in which you were treated — words and actions your conscious mind may have long ago forgotten or buried — despite any or all of these, you are a writer.

You *are* good enough. Your words are good enough. Your creations are good enough. Better than good enough. For they are the unique expressions of a unique heart that is, even now, opening to the prospect and possibility of finally being free to speak.

Feel that freedom. Open to that freedom. Embrace that freedom. It needn't frighten you. It needn't shut you down. It is safe. For in that freedom lies all the truth of the universe, just as within you lies all the truth of the universe.

So put pen to paper or let fingers dance upon the keyboard, and begin.

Begin at the beginning.

Let that first word be the God of the Old Testament, who allowed the world to form. "Let there be light," God said. Not, "I order and command light." Not, "The light must look a certain way, must be a certain brightness."

Creation is an act of allowing, of letting. *Let* there be light. *Let* there be creation. *Let* there be one story, then another. And let the words that best express that story find their way onto the page, without any need by you to intervene or get in the way.

Let. Let the words be. Let yourself be. There is no judging in the act of letting. There is no call to judge. There is no call to take any active role whatsoever. Surrender to creation and let it be.

God didn't say as the earth formed, "You know, I don't like this island over here and that mountain over there." God allowed the earth to form and saw it, and it was good. God didn't judge it to be good. By allowing, it *was* good. Inherently good.

Allow your creations to form without judgment, and they, too, will be good.

Give your creations life. Then give them the free will to form as they will, to live their imperative.

Let. Let them form. Let them be. Let them love you. Let yourself love them back. There is no need to judge. There is never any need to judge. Let the words flow, and let judgment go. Let it fly...far, far away where it can do no more damage or harm to you or your words or your work. Or to anyone or anything.

Now, pick a word, any word.

Let a word or phrase bubble up into your consciousness. A word that expresses your state of beingness in this moment.

Don't judge it. Never judge. Don't censor it. Never censor. Allow. Simply allow.

And when that word or phrase has emerged, let that be your starting point, your launching pad, your rocket, propelling you to the farthest reaches of the universe in a free-flowing, effortless flight of creation.

And so, write. Right now.

Remember to keep your pen moving across the page. Remember to let it move across the page. Free it and it will free you.

Let it fly, and let yourself fly with it.

If you feel stuck, keep going. Repeat. Free-associate. Write nonsense. Breathe. Doodle. Any or all of these will release the stuckness and propel you forward.

Write for as long as you can, until you feel complete...and then for a bit longer if that feels right.

Write. Now.

9. Strip Off Your Straitjackets

Free yourself from *all* preconceptions regarding genre, form, structure, content, audience or market. Don't force your words into the straitjacket of your preconceptions. Don't fence them in. Start writing and let your words take on the form that is theirs. Abandon all preconceptions, and free your story to live its full potential through you, a potential your conscious imagination can only begin to touch.

Revelations on the Muse Stream

I rarely know what my books will be about when I start writing them. All I know as I begin is that I *am* writing. What emerges might be a book. It might be a screenplay. It might be a form that's new to me. Or a genre I've never written in. It might be what my conscious mind thinks it ought to be. It might be what my conscious mind wants it to be. Ultimately, it will be what *it* needs to be, regardless of what I think or want.

All that matters is that I answer when my Muse calls. All that matters is that I get out of the way and let the Muse Stream take charge.

With four of my books, I wasn't even aware that I was writing a book when I started out.

I birthed my first, *The MoonQuest,* while leading a writing workshop. Back then, I never wrote during my workshops…not until that evening, at least, when an inner voice (my Muse?) insisted. What I ended up writing would become the opening of the first draft of a novel I knew nothing about.

If the unexpected fantasy that was *The MoonQuest* quickly identified itself as a book (even as it kept its plot to itself), *The Voice of the Muse: Answering the Call to Write* didn't even bother to tell me that.

It was a few years later and, with *The MoonQuest*'s early drafts completed, I was limping through the first draft of a sequel. When the words wouldn't come, which was often, I found myself penning handwritten reams of self-motivating vignettes; these would later form the foundation of *The Voice of the Muse*.

Then, there was *Dialogues with the Divine*, which I talk about in "Walk the Earth Naked, Clothed Only in Your Truth" under "Rule" #7.

More recently, my Facebook posts chronicling a challenging three-month period of mobile homelessness compiled themselves into *Pilgrimage: A Fool's Journey*.

Of course, not all my books have emerged that way. Yet even when I know something of a book's theme or subject, I rarely start with more than a title or with the vaguest hint of an idea. I just start, write on the Muse Stream and let the story reveal itself to me in the writing of it.

Do you know what *your* story is about? If you don't, the Muse Stream will reveal it to you, if you let it. If you do know it, that same free-flowing stream will get it onto the page for you — naturally, spontaneously and without struggle. Either way, the Muse Stream is waiting to help. All that's asked of you is to trust that. All that's asked of you is to surrender to it.

¶ *Read about the birth of "The MoonQuest" and experience the writing exercise that got it going in Section 9.*

It's All About Trust

Your story is a sentient entity, as I noted in "Writing into Uncharted Territory" ("Rule"#2), a sentient entity with a life force and wisdom of its own, with a will and imperative of its own. If you trust it to exercise that will and imperative through you, your writing experience will astonish you with its ease and free-flow. If you trust it to guide you through the journey of setting that wisdom onto the page, the story you have felt called to write will appear as if by magic.

Some writers fear that unless they retain an uncompromising grip on their creative experience, the resulting story will be disjointed, inconsistent, thematically uneven and structurally unsound.

I say: The more you abandon that all-too-human determination to control processes and predict outcomes and, instead, trust your story, the richer and more engaging will be your first — and final— draft.

Some years ago a visual artist came to me with the painter's equivalent of writer's block. She sensed a new style birthing through her but didn't know how to access it. All she could do was stare at her blank canvas in mounting frustration.

"Your only job is to hold the brush," I counseled her, "because that's the one thing your painting can never do on its own. If you get out of the way, abandon all preconceptions about what your work *should* look like and trust the brush to move your hand across the canvas, your painting will reveal itself to you."

She did, and it did.

It's no different with your writing.

In the end, the Muse Stream is about trust. It's about trusting that if you move from the driver's seat of your writing experience to its passenger seat, you will free onto the page a story that is more imaginative than anything you could have consciously thought up.

Creativity — and every writing experience is a creative process, regardless of genre, topic or type — is not a logical enterprise you can expect to control.

Creativity is about weird leaps of faith that often make no sense in the moment. In fact, what you judge to be nonsense as you write it may reveal itself to be the most brilliant aspect of your story by the time you type the final period on the final page.

When you let go all preconceptions and all expectations, you free your story to find the words, shape and form it needs, not the words shape and form you think it ought to have.

EXPLORATION

Ask yourself these questions in your *Writer's Block Unblocked* journal but don't think about the answers. And don't feel you have to answer each question independently if that doesn't feel right.

Let your individual answers (or whatever single answer these questions trigger) emerge freely and honestly, writing them on the Muse Stream in a free-flowing, stream-of-consciousness way where appropriate. Let yourself be surprised by the answers.

- What preconceptions about my story have I been clinging to? How can I let them go?
- Where am I being ruled by unreasonable, unhealthy or outdated expectations for my writing? Why do I feel attached to them? What steps can I take to detach from at least one expectation? What one step can I take right now?
- Where am I being ruled by others' expectations for me? Whose? Why do I feel attached to those expectations? What steps can I take to detach from at least one expectation? What one step can I take right now?

The Market Is Fickle: Ignore Today's Trends

Unless you have insider access to a breaking news story and can whip off a final draft in a few days, ignore today's market trends.

The themes, trends and topics that creative decision-makers seek today are unlikely to be the same ones they will be snapping up by the time you have finished your story. The market is volatile. Agents are inconsistent. Editors are fickle. Publishers are arbitrary. Producers are capricious. Today's trends rarely resemble tomorrow's. Or as Oscar-winning screenwriter William Goldman noted about the film industry, "Nobody knows anything." The publishing industry isn't much different.

On the other hand, what your heart calls on you to write in this moment may be what captures the attention of an agent, editor, publisher or producer in two months, six months or a year or two. The story your Muse sends you today may be the one that makes a publisher's or producer's pulse race when it crosses his or her desk some time after that.

Write what you must write right now, without expectations or preconceptions. And trust your story to find its right home in its right time.

10. Write

Write and let the words flow from your pen onto the page. Write and let the spirit of who you are emerge onto the page. All those things will happen the moment you unlock the gates that have kept the words, ideas, thoughts and feelings dammed up inside you. How? With the Muse Stream, which trains you to keep writing — through doubts, blocks, hesitation, fear and (seeming) unknowingness. Commit to the writer you are...and write.

Just Do It!

If "Write" seems the most obvious of my rules, it isn't. It's easy to put writing aside in favor of research. It's even easier to put writing aside while you try to figure out what this story that is calling to you is all about.

There is nothing to figure out. There is only this word...then this one...then this one.

Don't wait to figure out what your story is about. Don't worry about its direction, theme, structure or focus. Don't worry about scenes or chapter breaks. Don't worry about what people will think of it, or of you. Don't worry about audience or markets. Don't worry about anything. Set pen to paper or fingers to keyboard and, without judging or second-guessing what emerges, let your story do its wizardly work — on you as much as on the page.

Write what comes as it comes. Whatever it is. If you let its sentences flow freely through you and surrender to it unconditionally, you will learn all you need to know about your story through the writing of it.

Should your story's direction change along the way — or should its theme, structure or focus change — don't fight it. Surrender to the moment. Remember "Rule" #6? Surrender to the story you are writing in each moment. Your story knows what it's doing.

In other words: Write...the story you didn't know you had in you...the story you could never have imagined writing...the story you believed you could not write...the story that is yours alone to write.

11. Set Yourself Up for Success

If you're able to write only once a week, make that your goal and meet it. If you can set aside only ten minutes a month for writing, make that your goal and meet it. The easier your goals, the more likely you are to attain them. The more you do, the better you will feel about yourself and about writing. And the more you will write. Set yourself up for success, not for failure.

The Secret to Healthy Goal-Setting

Whenever I take on new coaching, consulting or mentoring clients, I always end our first session by asking, "How much time can you realistically devote to your writing over the next week?" Whatever the answer, I nearly always insist they cut it in half.

It's human nature to set overambitious goals. It's also what we're taught in school and what we're encouraged to do by most writing coaches, books, seminars and workshops and by most success programs.

Unfortunately, it's also human nature to judge ourselves harshly when we don't achieve those goals.

At best, when we miss our target, we hold to the original goal and try again. At worst, we lower our expectations. In neither case do we feel good about what we have accomplished. In both cases, we mourn our inadequacy rather than celebrating whatever it was we managed to write.

Isn't it better to set a goal that's easily achievable and reach it, rather than set a super-ambitious one and miss the mark? Isn't it better to set a one-page-per-week goal and get it done, rather than to aim for thirty and end up having written only one?

You may ask: "If the creative output is the same under both scenarios, what difference does it make?" The difference is how we feel about what we have accomplished...or failed to accomplish.

In the first situation, we feel sensational — about ourselves and about our writing. We feel as though we have succeeded.

In the second, we feel discouraged, and our perceived failure could continue to haunt and disable us as we move forward.

Set yourself up for success not for failure by giving yourself ridiculously easy goals and meeting them, easily. If that means committing to fifty words per writing session, that's fine. Set your goal and meet it. Then build on that success by gradually increasing your goal.

It's important to build up a sense of the possible, to continue proving to yourself that you *can* do it. Applying unrealistic goals that you fail to meet only underlines your challenges and fuels disappointment and discouragement. Instead, let each success breed more confidence and each confidence, more success.

Set yourself up for success, and before you know it, you will be dropping the ultimate period on the final draft of your story.

Oh, and don't forget to celebrate each success. That's what the next chapter is about.

Try This

Have you set yourself an overambitious writing goal that you are challenged to meet? It could be a word-count goal, or it could be a time goal. Whichever it is, cut it by half or more, enough that you can achieve it easily. As you meet your new goal, find a meaningful way to honor yourself for your success. Then increase the goal bit by bit, either from one day to the next or one week to the next.

Celebrate Every Success

I don't know whether it's human nature to dwell on what we haven't accomplished and to ignore or belittle our achievements, or whether we have been educated and socialized to do it. Regardless, we tend to spend much more time and energy on our perceived failures and missteps than on our successes.

That practice is not only counterintuitive, it's counterproductive.

That's because, as the maxim says, "energy flows where attention goes." In other words, the more we focus on our success, the more success we experience.

It stands to reason, then, that the most effective way to attract the success we desire is to focus on the successes we are already experiencing...to not only acknowledge them but celebrate them.

That's where your success diary comes in...

Your Success Diary

Starting tonight, let your final act before lights out be an inventory of your day's successes and accomplishments. Include your writing achievements, of course, but don't limit yourself to them.

Either run through them in your mind or, better still, record them in your *Writer's Block Unblocked* journal. Regardless, ignore anything you perceive as a failure, a setback or bad news. Pay no heed to any goal unreached, and disregard any task left undone. Forget recrimination, judgment and second-guessing. Don't compare yourself with anyone else.

Instead, acknowledge everything you achieved and any way in which you did not give up or give in to hopelessness or despair, however seemingly inconsequential it might in the moment seem.

Include any times when you followed your intuition or took a leap of faith. Writing on the Muse Stream is always a leap of faith.

Include acts of courage. Remember that courage is not synonymous with fearlessness. Courage is your ability to act in spite of fear. Writing from the heart and letting yourself be vulnerable on the page is always an act of courage.

Include everything.

No success is too insignificant to acknowledge. No achievement is too tiny to rejoice in. Celebrate that. Celebrate you!

Continue this inventory for at least as long as you're working with this book. And as the days progress, notice how your focus evolves from your perceived not-good-enoughs and failures toward your real successes and attainments, not only in your writing but in all aspects of your life.

Gold Stars

When I was a kid in grade school, we were given stickers and gold stars when we did well. Why? Because those acknowledgments inevitably fired us up to do even better. Incentives work. Meaningful incentives work.

What will your gold star be? What's your equivalent of the schoolroom sticker? How can you celebrate your writing success? How can you reward your creative achievements?

You don't have any, you say? I'm not talking about a publishing contract or a daily output of thousands of words. I'm not even talking about writing related to a specific project.

Did you write today? Anything? A chapter? A scene? A page? A paragraph? Then you have a success to celebrate.

Don't judge *what* you've written or how much you've written. Celebrate that you *have* written. (If you haven't written today, don't punish yourself; keep reading.)

Even if what you wrote won't be seen by anyone but you, it has value. Everything you write has value. Every word that finds its way onto the page, every draft that finds its way into the trashcan, every manuscript that fails to find a publisher — immediately or ever — has value.

If you didn't write today, don't beat yourself up. Celebrate the time you spent taking whatever steps you took to unblock your writer's block. Reading this chapter counts.

So, what will your gold star be for today's writing success? How can you reward yourself?

Your reward needn't be extravagant or expensive. It could be a specialty coffee at your favorite café, a book you've long coveted or any acknowledgment that is meaningful to you. Whatever your reward, let it be something special. However you earned it, celebrate it.

That's your reward for today, just to get a feel for the power of gold stars. But once your success diary has become a daily ritual, reward yourself weekly so that your gold star remains a special treat, not an everyday routine.

Remember to honor yourself, always, for meeting the challenge... whatever it is.

Celebrate your achievement. Energize your accomplishment. Give yourself a gold star.

12. Empower Yourself

This is *your* creative journey. Don't let anyone else take charge of it. Listen for the voice of your Muse as you leap, listen, surrender, trust and explore, as you rediscover the beauty and power of your words, your stories...your creativity.

The Past is Passed. Let It Go.

There's a coronation scene in *The MoonQuest* where King Fortas, having abdicated in favor of his son, Kyri, passes his crown, scepter, robe and other royal regalia to the young man. Kyri has no sooner donned the symbols of his father's kingship when the oracle presiding over the ceremony tells the prince to "let go all that encumbers him to the old reign."

As Kyri strips and each symbol of his father's monarchy is consigned to a burning pyre, the crowd chants, "The past is passed, we let it go."

Yet Kyri finds that he can't fully let the past go...can't fully let his father go...can't fully step into the new power that is his to claim. "You are not my subject," he says to the old man. "You are ever my lord."

Hearing this, the crowd grows restless, and its increasingly vocal chants calling for Fortas's reinstatement threaten the new reign before it has even begun.

"The past is not your lord," Fortas counsels Kyri. "Set your sights on the future, my son, my king. Set your sights on the future by seeing to the present. Don't let your vision linger longingly on the past. Let it go, my son. Let it all go."

Like Kyri, we disempower ourselves by clinging to any vestige of a past that no longer serves us. The past is passed, and by letting it go we, too, claim our sovereignty.

Let it go. Let it all go.

Exploration

Ask yourself these questions in your *Writer's Block Unblocked* journal but don't think about the answers. Let them emerge freely and honestly on the Muse Stream. Let yourself be surprised by the answers.

- Where in my creative life am I letting other people's ideas, ways of doing things and ways of viewing the world get in the way of discovering my own? Why am I making that choice? Those choices?
- Where is an unhealthy attachment to the past — to past ideas, past ways of writing, past ways of doing, past ways of being — preventing me from forging forward on new creative paths?
- What can I do, starting today, to free myself of past encumbrances and other people's ideas and ways of viewing the world to better chart an independent course in my creative life?

Your Words. Your Creative Journey.

Only you can write the story that is yours to write. And write it you must, regardless of the voices, inner and outer, that cry out for you to stop, that insist that they are trying to save you — from ridicule, from judgment, from shame.

There can be no salvation in stopping, in turning away, in listening to those voices — however sensible they might, in the moment, seem. Your sole salvation is the word that must emerge from the prison of your fear and into the light of your potential.

This word, now this one. And now this one.

Your words. *Your* creative journey.

One word following the next and the next, crashing through what you think you know — about yourself and the world — and carrying you into the Kingdom of the New, that wondrous realm beyond your conscious imagining that has been waiting for you since the beginning of time.

Just write. Just get words onto the page. It doesn't matter what you write or how you begin. All that matters is that you do begin. All that matters is that you write one word and then a second. Then a third.

Your words. *Your* creative journey.

However you begin, your first words will take you where you need to go, as long as you answer the call of your Muse, as long as you listen to *your* story, as long as you free your words onto the page and go wherever they carry you.

There is a time to revise, rework and reword. That time is later. Now is the time to write, to begin.

Have you begun? Are you writing your story, your poem, your book? Your screenplay, your stage play, your essay? Your song?

If not, close this book and open your writing app. Or get pen and paper. However you prefer to write, write. One word. Any word. Then another. And another.

It's time to begin. Now.

All it takes is the one word that gets you started.

Your word. *Your* creative journey.

Try This

Pick a word. Any word. It doesn't matter what it is. It doesn't even have to be a real word. Whatever it is, write it down. Don't judge it. Set it down on the page. Now another. If it follows logically from the first, that's fine. If it doesn't, that's fine too. Keep adding words to the first until a sentence pops into your head. Then do the same with your sentences until something more substantial emerges. Continue writing, on the Muse Stream, until you have gone as far as you think you can...then go farther still. Remember: All it takes is one word. *Your* word. So write and launch yourself onto a creative journey. *Your* creative journey.

12½. There Are No Rules

Forget your grade school teacher who was a stickler for spelling, punctuation and grammar. Forget your high school teacher who forced you to turn in an outline with your essay. Forget your college professor who insisted you write to a certain form or style. Forget the writers, classmates and instructors who cruelly critiqued or ridiculed you for "doing it wrong." Forget every writing guide and how-to you have ever read (including, where appropriate, this one). Forget everything you think you know about writing, and ignore anyone and everyone who tells you not only how to write but what to write.

When it comes to creative endeavors of any kind, there are no rules, musts or shoulds. There never can be. Why is that? Because if you're following someone else's rules, musts or shoulds, you're doing what has been done before, not blazing new trails…which is what creativity is all about.

Even these 12½ "rules" aren't rules. They are guidelines that have worked for me and for my students and clients on writing projects of all kinds and in all media and genres. But they're not gospel. Play with them. Adapt them. Make them yours. Remember: The only right way is the way that works for *you* — now.

I Did It My Way…and It Paid Off!

A year and several screenplay drafts after I broke all traditional screenwriting rules and adapted *The MoonQuest* for film my way (see "I Did It My Way" under "Rule" #1), I was at a book-signing for the novel when a woman strolled up to my table and picked up a copy of the book.

"You know," she said, once she had read the back cover blurb, "this might make a really good movie."

"Funny you should say that," I said as I signed her copy. "I've written a screenplay adaption."

"Funny you should say that," she countered. "I've just launched an independent film production company. I'm looking for projects." She glanced again at the cover. "If I like the book," she said. "I'll want to see your screenplay."

She loved the book and, to my amazement, the script. It, along with all my other *Legend of Q'ntana* stories, are now part of her slate of upcoming projects.

Forget the rules.

Try This

For this exercise, you will need lined paper and a pen, pencil, colored marker or other writing implement. Do your best to find lined paper, but it's okay to use unlined paper if you can't.

Turn your paper sideways, so that you are writing lengthways. On lined or "ruled" paper, you will be writing "against the rules." Even on unlined paper, you will be going against the established order. Be even more unconventional by writing with colored pencils or markers and/or by writing diagonally across the page, in spirals or in some other unorthodox way.

Make a list of as many of the perceived shoulds/musts/have-to's that are getting in the way of your writing as you can think of. Next to each, counter it with at least one way you can break that "rule."

Within the next twenty-four hours, break at least one of those "rules," then write about how that felt in your *Writer's Block Unblocked* journal.

5. Your Writer's Vision

There are no rules of architecture for a castle in the clouds.
G.K. CHESTERTON

Dreams come true. Without that possibility,
nature would not incite us to have them.
JOHN UPDIKE

What's Your Vision?

Sometimes when you're feeling stuck, it's because you lack a clear vision — for a project that isn't moving, for yourself as a writer or for your writing as a whole. One way to connect with and hold that vision is by crafting a vision statement that propels you into the energy of your day's writing and reminds you why you write or why you feel called to write, even if you're not currently writing.

In the same way a business crafts a mission statement to bring its goals into focus and to stay aligned with its aim and intention, a writer's vision statement can work similarly. It can be as brief as a sentence or as long as a page, or longer. It can speak in broad terms about your role as a writer, in detailed terms about a project or both. It's not something you think about or plot out. It's something you feel.

The vision statements I have created have often served as part of my gear-change from the outer to the inner, from mind-focus to Muse-focus. But they have performed their most valuable service on days when the words wouldn't come, when I was terrified of the words that wanted to come, when I doubted my ability or when I questioned the value of what I was writing or my value as a writer. On those days, my vision statements cut through my fear and resistance and returned me to center. They also ensured that all I wrote hewed as closely as possible not only to a writing project's true essence, but to mine.

How do you create a vision statement? Read on, first for examples of some of my vision statements, then for several ways you can craft your own, including a guided meditation.

My Vision

I have crafted many vision statements over the years, not only for my writing projects but for my vision of my "writer self." What follows are three examples: for my *Acts of Surrender* memoir, for my *Q'ntana* stories and for myself as the writer I am.

My *Acts of Surrender* Memoir

Acts of Surrender is an exploration for me and an inspiration for its readers.

It is designed to open readers to the possibilities of freedom in their own lives and to the gifts of surrender.

It's about a life not lived without fear but despite fear, a life lived in surrender to a higher imperative, a life lived as the Fool in the tarot lives: in faith, and trusting that all is good, all is safe and all is provided for.

As I write, I let my stories reveal their innate teachings through the telling of them.

My job is to keep interpretation to a minimum.

My job is to recount and relate, to reveal and recapitulate, to walk the earth naked once more, clothed only in the truths that have revealed themselves to me through the living of them.

I open my heart to this story, my story, more baldly and boldly told than through any parable, as powerful as such telling can be and is.

I open my heart and reveal my vulnerabilities and fears so that others may feel free to reveal and move through theirs.

Acts of Surrender is about the consciousness of freedom through surrender, awakening and revealing itself in the hearts of all those it touches.

My Legend of Q'ntana Stories

I had no concept of vision statements when I wrote "The MoonQuest," and I didn't craft this one until I was working on film adaptations of the first three stories. Now, because what was originally a trilogy has evolved into an open-ended series, the following has a permanent home on the wall above my desk, keeping me aligned not only with my vision for the series but with its vision for me.

These stories have always been bigger than me — from the moment the first one insisted itself onto the page.

These are stories that have so long been such a part of my life that it's as though they live deep within my cells.

I am every one of their characters, villain as much as hero, and have lived each of their joys, triumphs, disappointments, betrayals and disasters.

For decades, I have watched their themes play out in the world around me, just as I have experienced them play out in my life...and not always comfortably. In the end, I am more than the storyteller. I am the story.

Mark David Gerson: "The Writer I Am"

Perhaps the sentences I write are the seams that hold me together. Perhaps, that's the real reason I write. Perhaps, ultimately, it's the only reason.

Visioning Your Story

Creating a vision statement can be as simple as getting into a meditative space and writing on the Muse Stream from the key phrase, "My vision for myself as the writer I am is..." Or, "My vision for my writing as a whole is..." Or, "I am your Muse. My vision for you as the writer you are is..."

If you're working on a project, try one of these. "My vision for [*name of work*] is..." Or, "I am [*name of work*]. I am about..."

Another option is to ask yourself one or both of the following two questions. Don't use your analytical mind to figure out the answers. Instead, use your visionary mind to sense the answers, to feel the answers, to intuit the answers.

- What is my vision for my story?
- What is my vision for myself as a writer?

However you choose to proceed, write whatever comes to you — whether it speaks in metaphor, in general terms or with the most specific of detail. Length doesn't matter. Form and language don't matter. Your conscious mind's understanding of what you have written doesn't matter.

What matters is that, at some level, you and your creation sing the same song and that that harmony supports you not only as you write but through all your experiences as the writer you are.

If nothing comes right away, don't think or worry about it. Let the questions swirl around inside you as though you are sampling a fine wine. Let them steep within you as though you are brewing an exquisite tea. Meditate, go for a walk or do something else unrelated to your writing project. Clarity will come when it is ready...when you are ready.

Alternatively, use the "Your Vision Quest" meditation that follows.

Your Vision Quest

A Guided Meditation

Allow at least 45 minutes for this two-part meditation and for the writing experiences that flow from it.

My studio recording of this meditation is available for download or streaming as part "The Voice of the Muse Companion: Guided Meditations for Writers." See "Guided Meditations" in Section 1 ("Getting Started") to find out how to access the recording, as well as for tips on how best to use this book's meditations.

Part 1: Imaging Your Work

Relax. Close your eyes. Let your hands fall to your lap if you're sitting, to your abdomen if you're lying down. Breathe...deeply...in and out...in and out...in and out.

If you are setting off on this journey any later than first thing in the morning, run back over your day on fast-forward, and every time you get to something that was harsh or jarring, be it a thought, word or action — yours or someone else's — breathe in deeply and blow it out. As fully and noisily as you dare. As many times as you need to. Just blow it out.

And any moment that was especially wonderful, breathe it in deeply and reconnect with the energy of that.

Continue to breathe, deeply, and focus on your eyes.

If you wear glasses or contacts, imagine, for a moment, perfect vision without them. Imagine unassisted clarity without correction. Breathe into that.

See white light around your eyes and your third eye, that chakra or energy center that lies between your eyebrows and above the bridge of your nose. See that white light cleaning, clearing and cleansing any blurriness, fuzziness, distortion. Feel all veils being pulled away, one by one by one by one. As each veil dissolves, your vision becomes clearer and clearer and clearer.

Now, without removing all your attention from your eyes, move some of your focus to your heart. Be aware of the veils that surround your heart, whatever form they take.

Just be aware of them. Don't judge them.

Now, taking a deep breath, let the outermost veil fall away. Feel it fall away and dissolve. And when you breathe in again, notice that your heart feels lighter and freer and clearer. And as you breathe in again, another veil falls away. And another. And another.

Feel how much lighter your heart feels, how much freer your heart feels. It's okay if it feels a bit scary. Feel what you feel. And know that you are safe.

Keep breathing and feel yourself grow lighter and freer, lighter and freer, as you move closer to the heart of the matter and closer to who you are as the writer you are. And what a wondrous place that is.

Once more, breathe in, and if you sense another veil, breathe it away. And the next. And the next. And the next, until all that remains is a brilliant light, no longer veiled and dimmed, in your heart. Breathe into that and feel it.

Now, let the light from your eyes and the light from your heart connect in a ring of light that circulates energy from eyes to heart and around again. Either clockwise or counterclockwise; it doesn't matter. Whichever way it happens is perfect for you.

However the light moves for you, allow yourself to sense it, to feel it. Your vision and your heart as one.

Now, see a second ring of light, moving in the opposite direction from the first, this time connecting your heart to the hands resting on your lap or abdomen. Again, be aware of the circular motion of this circulating energy. Around and around. A constant and consistent river of radiance.

Connect the two rings, and you now have a figure eight or infinity symbol within you, as this inner light arcs from eyes to heart…heart to hands…hands to heart…heart back to eyes. And again. And again. And again, creating an infinite, luminous flow with your heart as its center.

As the energy circulates through that figure eight, be aware of the light pulsing in the topmost tips of your fingers, the hands with which you create, the hands that form part of the channel that brings your worlds into reality. Perhaps you feel the pulsing. Perhaps you don't. Whatever you feel physically, know that the energy is there, the light is there. The creative power is there — in your fingers, in your hands, in your eyes and in your heart, as the flow continues.

Sit with that flow for a few moments, feeling yourself immersed in its river of light and in the creative power that is moving through you.

Now, move your focus away from the infinity symbol and back to your eyes, your heart and your hands. Let a beam of light radiate from your eyes, another beam of light from your heart and a third beam of light from your hands — all meeting at a point in front of you, in front of your heart. That point in front of you, connected to you by all that light, is your work as a writer.

Perhaps it's your body of work. Perhaps it's a particular piece of work. Or a single aspect of your work. It doesn't matter. Whatever feels right in this moment, let that be whatever it is in this moment.

So your work stands separate from you but connected to you, in that space where all the beams of light meet right in front of you, in front of your heart. There is your writing.

I'm going to ask you some questions about your writing. I want you to allow the first answer that comes to mind to be the answer. And I want you to know that you will remember it long enough to put it on paper, if that is where it needs to go.

So, focusing the beams of light that travel from your heart, eyes and hands and onto that writing space in front of you...

- If your writing were a color, what color would it be? Just let the color come. Note it. Don't judge or analyze it. Be with it. Know that in this moment, that color represents your writing. Be with that color for a few breaths.

- Now, your writing is a space, shape or image. What is that space, shape or image? Again, don't judge or analyze. Let it be what it is. See it if you can. Note it. Know that this, too, you will remember long enough to write down or draw, if appropriate.

- Now, your writing is a sound. Music, perhaps. What kind of sound, what kind of music is it, for you, in this moment? Breathe into that sound. Be part of it and one with it. Let it surround you and enfold you, filling you with its melodies and harmonies, with its simplicity or complexity. That sound, however it is, whatever it is, is part of you. You will remember that, too, when and if it comes time to put it to paper...or to sing it, if that is how you choose to express it.

- Now, use your sense of smell. What does that tell you about your writing, about who you are as a writer? Is it a sweet smell? A smell that reminds you of something? Again, just be aware of it, and let it be.

- One more sense: What would your writing taste like, if you could taste it? Perhaps there's a particular food or type of food. Maybe it's a chocolate sundae, rich and creamy. Maybe it's comfort food — mashed potatoes and gravy. Maybe it's fresh, baked bread. Maybe it's a juicy pineapple. Maybe it's sweet and flowing like honey. Maybe it's spicy. Tangy. Tart. Let it be what it is. Acknowledge it. Be with it.

Now, go deeper still and let one word emerge that captures the spirit and essence of your work. Let it be the first word that comes, whatever it is. Don't judge it, don't analyze it. Don't second-guess it. If it makes no sense to your conscious mind, perhaps that's just as well. Let it be.

Now, staying in this meditative space that you're in, pause the meditation and jot down some notes about what you experienced — the color, the smell, the taste, the shape, the word...particularly the word.

Or take the word that just came to you and write on the Muse Stream from the phrase, "My writing [*or name of project*] is [*insert your word*]..." When you're done, put down your pen and, without reading what you have written, restart the recording, close your eyes and continue.

Part 2: Your Vision

Reconnect with that energy, that space. With that triangle, that pyramid of light. Again, feel the light connecting your eyes and heart and hands with your work, your work as the writer you are.

Now that you have experienced your writing from each of your senses, move your directed focus away from those specific senses.

Stand above them. Get an overview of all you experienced, all the different connections you felt with your writing through sensing your writing.

From that vantage point, look down at that space in front of you where you and your writing come together, and breathe into that space for a few breaths.

Feel the fullness of it and the vastness of it. The specifics of it, too. Feel all of it. Be all of it. Know all of it for the first time, again.

Feel, too, your connection with that part of you that is the writer and the writing and the work. Feel it and breathe into it. Breathe deeply into it.

Now, answer these questions — about your writing in general or about a particular writing project...

- What is it that, deep inside you, you want to convey through your work? First answer. No thinking about it. Let the answer come freely.
- What is it you want people to experience through your work? Again, go with whatever comes up first. Don't censor. Don't judge.
- What do you want people to experience of you through your work?
- What do you want people to experience of themselves through your work?

Open your eyes, again pause the meditation and jot down your answers to some of those questions, to whichever questions were answered.

Remember not to judge or analyze. Simply record your experiences, the answers you have received.

Stay in a meditative space and, when you're finished, resume the meditation.

Turn to a fresh sheet of paper. At the top of the page, write: "I, [*your name*], am a writer. Through my writing [*or the name of a work*], I..."

From that opening, write on the Muse Stream, letting what follows be as long or as short as it needs to be.

When you're done, sit quietly in the energy of that for a few minutes before reading it aloud. Feel free to revisit and revise this statement or series of statements as you, your project and your writing mature.

How to Use Your Vision Statement

Read your vision statement each time you sit down to write or when you're feeling stuck. Don't merely read it. Feel it. Embody it. Connect with it, and through it connect with the essence of your work.

If possible, read your vision statement aloud — with heart, power, confidence and intent. Thus empowered, the words of your vision statement will fuel and inspire you all the way to your final draft and beyond.

Read it again before sharing completed drafts with friends or colleagues, and hold to your vision when you receive feedback, criticism or reviews — positive or negative.

This vision, as embodied in and by your vision statement, will always keep you centered and aligned with the true heart of your work, with the true heart of the writer you are.

Note that your vision statement is not fixed in stone. As your project progresses and as you mature through the writing of it, you may choose to refine your vision statement to match new insights and awareness.

Try This

Keep a copy of your vision statement somewhere on your phone — in your note-taking or writing app or as a screenshot on your camera roll — so that you always have it with you. Also, record it into your phone so that you can listen to it while you're cooking, commuting, walking the dog, shopping or waiting in line.

¶ *See also Section 10, "Other Perspectives," for more about giving and asking for feedback and Section 11, "On Rejection, for more about handling harsh criticism or rejection.*

6. Busted: Seven Common Writers' Myths

Feeling is the power that drives art.
DAVID MILNE

When you write a novel, you write it all day long, not just when you're sitting behind your typewriter. You write it as you smoke a cigarette, as you eat lunch, as you make a phone call.
RAYMOND CHANDLER

The Myths

1. "I'm Blocked"

2. "I'm Easily Distracted"

3. "I Don't Have Time To Write"

4. "I Never Finish Anything I Start"

5. "I Don't Know How To Start or End"

6. "I Don't Know Anything About…"

7. "I'm Not Good Enough"

1. "I'm Blocked"

No, you're not. There is no writer's block. There is no need for a blank page to remain blank. There is no reason for words not to flow. They may not be the words you would choose from your personality mind. That is not a block. That's a choice.

Unfortunately, unless you allow the words that yearn to flow room and space, no others are likely to flow. No others worth mentioning. No others that will have the power and impact and emotion and life and heart and truth of those you denied an exit visa from your heart to the page.

Let them go. Let them free. Let yourself free. When you do, there are no blocks.

So, set the tip of your pen to the page or touch your fingers to the keyboard and begin. Simply begin.

Don't stop. Don't think. Don't question. Don't second-guess. Don't criticize. Don't judge. Don't censor.

Allow. Allow the pen to move you. Allow the keyboard to choose which keys you will press. Allow the words to flow. Allow them, and they will.

It may feel difficult at first. But the strain isn't your mind straining to find the right words. It's your brain straining to hold you back from the right words.

Don't let your mind stop you. Don't let anything stop you. Write any time and at all times. Write when you would rather be sleeping. Write when you would rather be doing laundry. Write when you would rather be doing your neighbor's laundry. Write whenever you feel the slightest resistance to writing. That resistance is the struggle of your words trying to surge past the barriers you have erected against them.

Tear down the barricades, just this one time. Tear them down and let the flow surge from you. Try it once. Then try it again. And discover that the block you thought you had has not dissolved because it was never truly there. The words were always there because the words are always there.

All you have to do is let them have sovereignty over you. Give them the keys to the kingdom of your dreams, your visions, your truth. They will not let you down. They may surprise you. They may scare you. They *will* empower you.

¶ *See also Myth #1 in Section 7.*

2. "I'm Easily Distracted"

"Writers," writes Andrew J. Fenady in his novel *A Night in Hollywood Forever*, "never want to work, never. They all find any excuse not to sit down and look at an empty sheet of paper or a blank monitor — the room's too hot or too cold — they have to go to the toilet — pencils need sharpening — the typewriter needs a new ribbon — the keyboard needs cleaning — the pictures on the wall need straightening — the wastebasket needs to be emptied — or it's lunchtime." Although Fenady may be speaking only for his book's main character, a detective-turned-non-productive-novelist, distraction is an issue that, at one time or another, keeps most writers away from their pens or keyboards.

Between the real demands of family, doing whatever you must to pay the bills, keeping up with the marketing demands that now face every writer, handling the manufactured demands inventoried by Fenady and the ambivalence many of us sometimes feel toward the act of writing, it's a wonder that any words ever make their way onto anyone's page.

If you have heard yourself think or utter any of the following seven excuses, you are probably dealing with the kind of distraction or procrastination that feeds your resistance and prevents you from moving forward with your writing.

Seven Common Excuses for Delaying (or Avoiding) Writing

All the following begin with this phrase: "Before I can start writing, I must..."

1. Check my email, voicemail or social media accounts and/or deal with a text message, email, social media post or app notification, or make a phone call.

2. Make a cup of coffee or tea or get one from my favorite café, or make a snack or run to the store to get one. Or both.
3. Watch one more episode of [*insert favorite video or streaming series*] or play one more game of [*insert favorite game*].
4. Clean the bathroom, run the dishwasher, do laundry, wash the car…or all of these.
5. Take a nap.
6. Google my topic. Or look up the average temperature on Neptune (-353° F) or the capital of Mongolia (Ulaanbaatar). Or do some other kind of research unrelated to anything I'm working on. Or reorganize my project files.
7. Wait for my Muse to show up.

If you find yourself putting anything ahead of the blank page, you're not alone. Writers often have the cleanest cars, floors, fridges and toilets, the best grasp of useless trivia, the most up-to-date filing systems or the best record for returning calls or emails because nearly any task can seem more palatable than sitting down to write. If any of this sounds like you, here are seven surefire tips for minimizing distraction and procrastination until you have completed your day's writing…or, at least, a first installment of your day's writing…

Seven Tips for Minimizing Distraction and Procrastination

1. Go Offline

If you must be online because your writing app or document is in the cloud, do your best to keep all online distractions out of sight and earshot until after you have written. *All!* That includes any on your mobile devices as well as those on your computer. Start by muting/hiding all notifications, and unless you write using a browser-based app, quit your web browser. If possible, disable autocorrect, spellcheck and grammar check while you're writing. Also, quit your email app and stay away from all social media. While you're at it, enable your phone's "do not disturb" setting. Better yet, turn on airplane mode or power your phone down altogether. *Treat your writing time as sacred.*

2. Plan Your Snacks

Get your coffee/tea and treats ready *before* you sit down to write. Alternatively, make snack prep part of your transition ritual. (See "Seven Surefire Tools for Transition" under Section 8's Surefire Solution #3.) Another option is to make a coffee break your reward for reaching a pre-determined milestone toward the day's writing goals. *Treat your writing time as sacred.*

3. To Everything There Is a Season

This is not the season to catch up on your DVR'd TV shows, binge-watch your favorite streaming series or play a favorite video game. Nor is it the season to pick up that book you're a few pages from finishing or that magazine article you're nearly done with. It's the season to write. *Treat your writing time as sacred.*

4. Cleanliness May Be Next to Godliness... but Creativity Is Godly

Steer clear of sponges, mops, feather dusters and cleaning rags. Don't go near the Windex or all-purpose cleaner. Ignore the dishes piling up in your kitchen sink and the laundry overflowing your hamper. If your toilet is revolting, let it stay revolting for a few hours more. There is only one thing to do, and you know what it is: Write, right? *Treat your writing time as sacred.*

5. Use Writing Time for Writing

As essential as research, organization, filing and related support tasks may be to your project's completion, don't let them intrude on your writing time. Set aside a separate time for non-writing tasks. *Treat your writing time as sacred.*

6. Ignore Faux Fatigue

Does a wave of exhaustion sometimes wash over you when you sit down to write? There's a good chance that you're not really tired but that fear and resistance are masquerading as physical fatigue. Instead of fleeing to your bed or the sofa for some shut-eye, start writing on the Muse Stream. Once you're in the flow, your drowsiness may disappear.

7. Don't Wait for Your Muse

Your Muse never needs an invitation and is never late for an appointment. How can it be when it is always present? Similarly, your Muse will never abandon you. Nor will it ever stop listening to you. Sit down, get one word onto the page, open your heart and mind, and your Muse will deliver. Always.

If keeping distraction and procrastination at bay has proven impossible, keep pen and paper or your laptop or mobile device by your bed, and don't get up until you have written. That's how I got through the initial third of my first drafts of *The MoonQuest* and *The StarQuest*.

With *The MoonQuest*, I was so stressed by the notion of surrendering to the story (even though I was already teaching the philosophy), that I stayed in bed until I had achieved my morning's writing goal.

With *The StarQuest*, as I explain in "How I Found the Time to Write" (see Writer's Myth #3), I also stayed in bed. However, that was because, with limited time each day to write, those early morning moments were the only ones that were stress-free, distraction-free and exhaustion-free. Writing also set the tone for the day ahead, filled as it was with a job I hated.

Another benefit of making writing your first assignment of the morning (apart from getting it done) is that you won't waste time through the rest of your day collecting meaningless distractions to avoid having to write.

Try This

What kinds of distractions do you typically succumb to? What's your favorite form of procrastination? Make a list of all distractions and procrastinations that have kept you from writing over the past seven days. Include distractions that have delayed or shortened your writing time. Don't judge yourself or be hypercritical. Instead, notice all the energy you have put into *not* writing.

When you have completed your list, close this book, free yourself of all potential distractions, open a fresh page in your writing app (or pick up pen and paper), and write.

Anything.

Just do it.

Now.

Put Away Your Journal

Journals can be wonderful tools for clearing our minds of the emotional sludge that prevents us from writing. That's why I urged you to keep one as you work through this book.

Unfortunately, journals can also be distractions, gobbling up so much writing time and energy that there's none left for your creative projects.

What if you took the anxiety that seems to be blocking you and, instead of dumping it into your journal, channeled it into a new or existing story? What if you let one of your characters take on your fear?

I was about a hundred manuscript pages into my first draft of *The MoonQuest* when my life turned itself — and me — upside-down. As I write in *Acts of Surrender: A Writer's Memoir*, I found myself selling off most everything I owned, buying my first car at age thirty-nine and leaving Toronto, my home for eleven years, with my few remaining possessions crammed into my Dodge Caravan. Destination: three Canadian provinces and a thousand miles away in Nova Scotia, where I knew no one and was set to birth a new life. Packed away in the bowels of my minivan were my *MoonQuest* notes and pages.

Through the two months between my arrival in my new home and the day I dared pick up my *MoonQuest* manuscript, I journaled feverishly. Obsessively. Two, three, sometimes four times a day. With little else going on in this new life and few distractions, I had nothing else to do. Besides, I was scared, mostly of the void I had created. What I wasn't doing was working on *The MoonQuest*.

One day in my journal, I found myself writing, "Put away your journal." I was resistant at first, yet I soon realized that I had been using my journal as a crutch, not as a tool. Within a few weeks, I was back at work on *The MoonQuest*, letting Toshar, the book's main character, take on my angst.

Allow your journal to be a tool, not a crutch. Use it to explore, not to escape. Let the emotions you would release onto your journal pages express instead through your characters, your setting, your plot. Transform your anger into a scene, your fear into description, your anguish into dialogue. You don't write fiction and don't want to start? Channel your distress into an essay, blog post or memoir chapter.

Your journal has its place. Use your discernment to determine what that place is from day to day, and don't let it stop you from moving forward with your creative projects.

Try This

Next time you feel stressed and anxious — or joyful and exhilarated — don't reach for your journal. Reach instead for a blank sheet of paper and write about all you are experiencing — not as yourself but as a fictional character. Use the first person. Then do it again, in the third person. Do it a third time from a man's point of view if you're a woman, from a woman's if you're a man.

What about right now? How are you feeling right now? Put that emotion, whatever it is, into an existing project. If you have none, let that feeling kick off a fictional journey on the Muse Stream. Pick a name, any name, male or female, and invest that character with the emotions bubbling or roiling within you. Add a second character, and transform one character's soliloquy into a scene.

Distraction Happens

When you carry the world in your pocket and on your wrist, as most of us do these days, it's hard not to be distracted when that world pings, rings, buzzes, hums and vibrates at you constantly. Even should you manage to avoid the online distractions that are nearly always on your person, many of those same distractions show up when you're on your computer. Whether it's emails, text messages or app notifications, it can be hard to stay focused when family, friends, work, your favorite social media, your favorite stores and your favorite games are all vying for your attention. Then there are the offline distractions, a similarly endless list that includes pets, kids, spouses, doorbells, street noise, growling stomachs and coffee addictions.

Let's face it. Distractions happen. Connections weaken, waver and snap. The tiniest interruption, even a fly buzzing in front of the computer screen, can sever our focus and abort our flow.

Some days, we can recover from the distraction in an instant. Some days, recovery feels impossible.

When distraction disrupts your flow, stop and sit with nothing but your breath. Focus on the air as it enters and leaves your lungs. Focus on your chest as it rises and falls. Focus on the silences as they ebb and flow.

Take however long you need to breathe out the distractions and breathe in to your inner creative space, to the voice of your Muse, to the writer you are.

Consider, also, a meditative walk. Often a quiet break from desk, page or computer is all that is required to realign your focus and reconnect you with the heart of your writing and the writings of your heart.

If, in the end, you are unable to restore your connection and flow, don't punish yourself. Accept the gift of whatever you managed to write...and know that more words will flow, yet more freely, next time.

3. "I Don't Have Time To Write"

Yes, you do. Through the Muse Stream exercises in previous sections, you have already discovered how much you can write in twenty or thirty minutes. Who can't set aside twenty minutes a day — or every few days — to write. Twenty minutes is more than you can manage? How about fifteen?

When Connie Willis quit her teaching job to raise her daughter, she decided that it was time to start writing professionally, because that was something she could do at home.

What Willis discovered was something radically different. "I never had, for the next eighteen years, more than fifteen minutes at my disposal," the fantasy/sci-fi author would later reveal in a TVOntario interview, "and I learned that if I really wanted to be a writer, I couldn't wait until I had more than fifteen minutes at my disposal."

Willis learned to write in whatever odds and ends of time showed up for her: in the orthodontist's waiting room, at football and basketball games, in the car outside her daughter's school, at her husband's gymnastic class. Her strategy paid off. Now with dozens of novels and short stories to her credit, Willis has won more major science fiction awards than any other writer: eleven Hugos and seven Nebulas.

"You've got to write today," she continued, "when you have the time that you have."

The same is true for you. There is always time. Seek it out.

Where Does the Time Go?

Too often we labor under the false assumption that we have no time to write, that our lives are too busy with work, family or other responsibilities. "I'll wait until the kids grow up and are out of the house," we say.

Or, "I'll do it when I retire." Why wait until more than half your life is over to start living your writing dreams?

Like Connie Willis, you *do* have the time to write, even in the midst of the overwhelming calendar of obligations and commitments we all juggle every day. How do you find that time? By becoming conscious of the ways you spend your time.

For each of the following activities, estimate (honestly!) a weekly average in your *Writer's Block Unblocked* journal. Why weekly? Because for most of us, not all days are created equal. (Don't worry: I'm not going to ask you to give up any of these pursuits.)

How much time each week do you spend…

1. Watching TV?
2. Watching Netflix? Other streaming services?
3. Reading newspapers/magazines (online and/or in print)?
4. On mindless online distractions, including random Googling and/or browsing?
5. On social media?
6. Watching YouTube? Other videos?
7. Playing video and/or other online games?
8. On other non-essential activities on any electronic device?
9. At the gym?
10. On dinner, coffee and/or drinks with friends?
11. On movies, live theater, museums and/or galleries?
12. On reading for pleasure?
13. Going to clubs?
14. Going to sporting/athletic events, not including those events your kids or other family members are competing in?
15. Commuting (not in a car you're driving)?
16. On other pursuits and activities, online or off, that you can honestly categorize as needless, superfluous, distracting, time-wasting or otherwise non-critical?

I promised I wouldn't force you to sacrifice any non-writing activities. So here's what I want you to do:

Take each of your totals and divide it by five, six or seven for a daily average per activity. Then divide each of those totals by half; one half stays with the activity, and the sum of the remaining halves is allocated to writing. Can you free up that time every day to devote to writing? No? What if you were to divide your weekly totals by a third? By a quarter?

Note that when it comes to #15 (commuting time), there is nothing you need to give up. All I ask is that you devote some of that travel time to writing.

EXPLORATION

Ask yourself these questions in your *Writer's Block Unblocked* journal and answer honestly:

- How can I make writing a priority in my life?
- What's my realistic commitment to my writing?
- How much time will I devote to my writing today? Tomorrow? Next week?

¶ Revisit "Rule" #11 ("Set Yourself Up for Success") in Section 4.

How I Found the Time to Write

It's November 2008. The global economy is crashing, and so is mine. As a fifty-four-year-old writer and spiritual wanderer with no recent stable employment history, I have limited prospects, and the one job I am able to land is at crafts chain Hobby Lobby as perhaps the world's oldest stock boy. The pay doesn't cover my living expenses, the hours are long, and I hate it. Some days I'm grateful, some days I'm angry. Most days, all my muscles ache as I crawl into bed soon after dinner.

My friends are sympathetic, but only one offers a suggestion: "Write, write, write," he urges in an email. "It is your soul work. It is your gift."

As I read his words over and over, sobbing, I recall a recent commitment I made to myself, that after a decade of fits and starts, it's time for me to complete my second novel, *The StarQuest*. "Regardless of what it takes and what is required of me," I remember declaring, "I commit to getting it done. It's time, and I'm ready."

Now, I resolve, I have no choice but to act on that commitment — not only because I owe it to myself but because it's the only thing that will give meaning to days that feel increasingly meaningless.

Now, at a time when it feels as though I have no time, I must somehow make time to write daily, something I haven't done since the earliest drafts of *The MoonQuest*.

But how? And when? Should I aim for mornings or evenings? What time should I start? What time should I end?

I have always been slow to get going first thing in the day, and mornings have never been my best time. Yet, I made it through the first draft of *The MoonQuest* by working on it as soon as I woke up, before I could create any excuse to procrastinate. Mornings would be tough, but evenings after work would be tougher.

Okay, I say, I will commit to mornings. But how early do I need to start? I know many job-bound writers get up at four or five in the morning. Might that work for me? I want to think that it will, but I know myself better than that. It probably won't work more than once. Maybe twice.

If four or five in the morning isn't sustainable, I ask myself, what is? How can I do what I coach my clients to do? How can I create a realistic schedule that I will stick to? How can I set achievable goals that I will meet? How can set myself up for success?

The answer I ultimately come up with feels lame at first: I decide to set my alarm for a quarter to seven instead of for seven, and to write in bed during those fifteen minutes. As pointless as a fifteen-minute writing session initially feels, it works — on multiple levels. Not only am I making progress on *The StarQuest* for the first time in years, but when I leave for work each morning, I feel more positive and optimistic than I have felt in weeks. Even better is that by July, after two false starts, the first dating back more than ten years, I finally complete a first draft of *The StarQuest*.

Now Is the Time to Write

Don't wait. Don't wait for the perfect moment or the perfect slice of time. Don't wait for your vacation. Don't wait to fix up a special place in your home. Don't wait until your spouse is away on business. Don't wait until you finish this paragraph.

Is your pen in hand? No? Pick it up. Turn to a fresh page in your notebook. Touch the nib to the writing surface. Write a word. Any word. Whatever flows from your pen. Don't think about it. Don't think about anything. Just write that one word. Then another. Then another.

No pen? Do the same thing with your computer…or your tablet…or your smartphone. Do it now.

The best time to write is now. The only time to write is now. All you need is twenty minutes. Even ten will do.

You don't know what to write? Pick a word or phrase from "Seventy Keys to Unlock Your Writing" in Section 3. Any one.

Pick it.

Write it.

Now.

Then keep going.

Don't stop…not for any reason. Keep placing one word after the next after the next after the next, until you're done.

How Much Did You Write?

How much did you write? How many words did you squeeze into those ten or twenty minutes? No, don't stop and count. Simply be aware of the volume. Don't stop to reread or judge the quality; simply notice the quantity. Now, can you honestly say that you lack the time to write? How can you claim that when twenty minutes has wrought such output?

There is always time to write. There may not be as much as you would prefer. It may not appear in convenient places. But it's there. Waiting for you.

You can't find twenty minutes? Surely, you can find ten in the interstices of life — while you're waiting in the doctor's office, while you're riding public transit or during a lull at work. Carve it out of your lunch hour. Wake up ten minutes earlier. Go to sleep ten minutes later. The time is there. And the words, once you demonstrate your willingness to receive them, will cooperate if you allow them to free-flow from your pen on the Muse Stream.

"Wait," I hear you say, "I don't write longhand. I can't read my handwriting. I can't write unless I'm on a computer."

Do you have a tablet or smartphone? Use that.

Your cellphone isn't a smartphone? Call your voicemail and leave yourself a message with thoughts and ideas about your current project.

Train yourself to write on anything, with anything, anywhere. Familiarize yourself with the native note-taking applications on your phone and tablet, or seek out apps better-suited to your needs. If you tend to move between devices, use a cloud-based app to ensure that your jottings are available on all your devices.

Chances are, your phone is with you all the time, so make it your go-to note-taking tool. And as the best ideas seem to show up inconveniently in the middle of the night, consider having your phone on your nightstand when you go to bed.

Alternatively or as a supplement, keep a pen and notepad in your pocket, purse, briefcase or backpack; keep another in your car's glove compartment and another by your bed.

Remember: The words long to pour from you. Never doubt that. They yearn to spill from your heart onto the page. They don't need to wait for the right tool, the right time or the right place. You may think you need the right tool, the right time and the right place. The words don't. The moment you open to them, wherever you are, whatever you're using, they will come. Always.

What if ten minutes is more than you can manage on a given day? First, don't beat yourself up. Don't judge yourself as uncommitted or unworthy. Instead, take five minutes, or two minutes or thirty seconds. Take that time and connect with the writer you are, connect with the project you are working on, connect with the project you have not yet begun. Read your vision statement. The simple act of connecting with the spirit of your writing endeavor will serve you in powerful ways.

¶ *Haven't crafted a vision statement yet? Skip back to Section 5 and do it now.*

4. "I Never Finish Anything I Start"

Perhaps you never have...yet. That doesn't mean you can't. Perhaps you have yet to start something you care enough about to see to completion. Perhaps you have been writing about things that seem like good ideas but aren't *right* ideas — ideas that excite you, that fire you up, that by their very nature keep you *wanting* to write. If you're searching for a surefire way to get stuck in your writing, choose themes, topics and stories you're indifferent about.

Another reason for abandoning works-in-progress can be fear. If you let it, as I did for decades, your fear will paralyze you.

You may not be able to dissolve your fear, but you can write about the fear. You can write through the fear. You can write past the fear.

¶ *See also "Write the Fear" under Surefire Solution #1 in Section 8 and "Is Your Write Idea the Right Idea for You?" under Surefire Solution #6.*

The Breath of Creativity

Are you breathing? In your terror, have you forgotten to breathe? Writing at its truest is an act of meditation. And meditation, whatever the form, relies upon breath.

Are you stuck? Does word not follow word with ease? Does fear poke its pointy head between one word and the next?

Breathe.

Write "I am breathing" and breathe that sentence onto the page as you write it. Then exhale, "I am breathing out." All of it onto the page, in alignment with your breath.

Breathe out the fear and breathe in the story. Breathe out the stuckness and breathe in a clear path to the next word, whatever it may be.

Writing — as all creativity, as all life — is an act of allowing. Allow your breath to come, allow your breath to go. Be conscious of each intake and outflow. Become conscious by writing the words of your breath onto the page: "I am breathing in...I am breathing out."

Keep breathing. Keep writing your breath, the breath of creativity. And in no time your breath will return to its normal unconscious practice, as will the outpouring of words.

Breathe, for in your breath resides your life. In your breath, too, resides your story. Breathe your words onto the page and breathe life into your words. Do that and the story will take care of itself.

Try This

When you find yourself with no next word to write, remember that each breath you breathe comes naturally, without thought or forcing. Write as you breathe, knowing that the moment you get out of the way — out of *your* way — word will follow word, just as breath follows breath. Write as you breathe: freely, unconsciously, unselfconsciously, flowingly, and you will find your way to the next word and the next and the next...all the way to the end of your story.

5. "I Don't Know How to Start or End"

Of course, you know how to start. That's what the Muse Stream is all about. You don't have a theme, topic or opening? Pick a word, any word, and start. Keep writing without stopping, and *don't think*.

You don't know how it's going to end? You don't have to. Perhaps it's even better if you don't. Regardless, all you need to know in this moment is the next word. Only one word. Any word. It doesn't even matter what that word is. If you write on the Muse Stream, if you trust, if you put your faith in the superior wisdom of your story and surrender to that story, that one word will take you where you need to go. Always.

Your sole responsibility — your *soul* responsibility — is to begin. So begin. Your sole responsibility is to continue. So continue.

Drop a word onto a page. Then another. And another. Follow the words where they take you. Let them open up into sentences and paragraphs as they reveal your story to you...the story only you can write. Remember "Rule" #3? Leap into the void...and trust.

As you move forward, remember that your page is blank for a reason. It's waiting for your creation, for the voice of your Muse to push, cajole, sweet-talk, threaten or charm you into filling it. You will fill it more quickly, easily, naturally and spontaneously if you surrender — to the Muse Stream ("Rule" #5) and to your story.

Your Story Is Waiting for You

Your story is waiting for you. It's waiting for you to notice it, waiting for you to catch up with it, waiting for you to surrender to it.

Perhaps you know what that story is. Perhaps you have been unable to start it. Perhaps you have started it but found yourself mired in stuckness, spinning your creative wheels and unable to move forward.

It doesn't matter. What matters is that you acknowledge that your Muse is trying to get your attention. What matters is that you open your heart and blank page to it. What matters is that you surrender.

I didn't know anything about a book called *The MoonQuest* when its words began to flow through me. All I knew was that my Muse was calling me and that the only way to answer that call was to write.

As I wrote, the story took care of itself. One day's writing led to the next. One draft led to the next. Each day and draft drove my pen. My pen, in turn, drove me. My only job was to release all attachment to form, structure, content and outcome. My only job was to write and let the words go where *they* chose and create what was theirs to create.

As it turned out, they chose to create a book I never planned to write.

The StarQuest was different. Even before I finished *The MoonQuest*, I knew *The StarQuest* was in me, waiting to emerge. I knew it was a book. I even knew the tiniest smidge of its story before I began.

So how did I begin?

The same way I begin every piece of writing: by beginning. Whatever you know of your story, you start every piece of writing the same way, with a single word. With a single letter. With a single pen stroke or keystroke.

Any word. Any letter. Any pen stroke or tap on the keyboard.

"In the beginning was the Word. And the Word was with God..."

Your first word also resides with God or your Muse or whatever creative source you acknowledge. So does your second and third and thirtieth and thirty-thousandth.

Whichever word gets you started is the right one. And that right one will inexorably lead you to the next and the next and the next. And the next. If you let it.

Ultimately, all those words will lead you through your story to its ending, an ending that has been waiting for you since the beginning of time. Of course, it has. For your story has existed since the beginning of time, waiting patiently for you to acknowledge it, open your heart to it and capture its essence in words on a page or screen.

Are you ready to acknowledge it? Then pick up your pen or touch your fingers to the keyboard and free a word onto the page.

You're not sure where your story will take you? If you listen, it will tell you. If you surrender, it will guide you. If you let it, it will write itself.

6. "I Don't Know Anything About..."

You already know everything you need to know — at least all the important things. Anything else can be uncovered through research.

What do I mean?

It's not your detailed knowledge or inside information that will touch your readers, that will move them to deeper places within themselves. Only your emotions can do that.

Whoever we are, wherever we're from, whatever our religion, sexual orientation, ethnic identity, cultural background, national origin or skin color, we all share one thing: our humanity. And as human beings, we all draw from the same pool of human emotion.

If you can give yourself permission to tap into that pool within you, you will always write not only what you know but what others want most to know from you: the truths of your soul.

When I tell you to write what you know, I am not telling you to write about the superficialities of your experience. I am telling you to write what you know in your deepest heart. To write your fire. To write your joy. To write your pain. To write your truth.

The only knowledge that is unique to you is the knowledge of your heart, the wisdom of your soul, the force of your passion. Write from those places that no one else can, and you will touch readers in ways that no one else can.

Write What You Know...If You Dare

How often have you been told to "write what you know"? How often have you stifled your creativity because you don't know enough to "write what you know"? How often have you said something like...

I can't write about someone who's twice my age...or half my age.

I can't write about a black man because I'm not black...or a man. I can't write about women if I'm a man.

I can't write about pilots; I don't know how to fly and I've never been in a cockpit.

I can't write about a priest, rabbi, mullah or minister because I'm an atheist.

I can't write about a gay man, transgender individual or lesbian because I'm none of those.

I can't write about someone who's liberal because I'm conservative (or vice versa).

I can't write about someone who comes from a different background, culture or country.

Of course, you can.

You say you can't write about a cleric's faith because you don't believe in God. Have you never had faith in someone or something? Do you have faith that the sun will rise tomorrow or that spring will follow winter? At its core, faith is faith, however it's expressed. And whatever the particulars of its cause, every crisis of faith sparks a similar emotional response.

So you have never experienced the discrimination or betrayal a black woman, gay man or transgender individual might have felt? Have you ever been attacked for who you are? Have you ever been denied what you believed was rightfully yours? Have you ever felt your personhood and humanity under attack? Have you ever felt betrayed?

No? Think back to your childhood. Think back to the emotions of childhood, to the bullies in the schoolyard, to the adults who criticized you...who betrayed you. Do more than think back. Relive and reexperience those emotions.

You have lived at least some of those same emotions you feel you dare not describe in someone else.

Accept the dare. Step up to the challenge. You owe it to yourself at least to try. For if any character — however far removed from your life and lifestyle — comes to you and demands that his or her story be told through you, then all you can do is trust that whatever you need lies within you.

Of course, research may be required. Remember, though, that unless you're writing a dry recitation of history, it is the emotions that will touch your readers, that will affect them, that will move them to deeper places within themselves. And we all — whether we're black, white, green or purple — draw from the same pool of emotions.

If you can give yourself permission to tap into that pool within you, you will always write what you know. For all you need to know lies inside you. Now. In this moment.

Go ahead and write what you know...if you dare.

Try This

Write on the Muse Stream from any or all of these key phrases:

- I know fear...
- I know humiliation...
- I know betrayal...
- I know what it feels like to be different...
- I know what it feels like to be attacked...
- I know what it feels like to feel trapped...
- I know what it feels like to be judged...
- I know what it feels like to be shamed...
- I know what it feels like to betray...
- I know what it feels like to attack...
- I know what it feels like to judge...
- I know what it feels like to shame...
- I know what it feels like to humiliate...
- I know what it feels like to lose faith...
- I know what it feels like to...

Let it be a story from your childhood, from your adolescence or from your present. Or let it be a creation of your inner vision. Whichever it is, write what you know, from your heart. Surrender to that knowingness and let the true emotions, true passion and true truth of your soul be unleashed onto the page.

7. "I'm Not Good Enough"

This is the biggest myth of all. You *are* good enough. You are good enough because everyone is good enough. Everyone carries the seeds of creation within them. Instead of viewing yourself as less than in relation to others, see yourself in each moment as the perfect expression of your divine essence and soul's imperative. When you do that, you will realize that all comparisons are irrelevant. And if all comparisons are irrelevant, you can't *not* be good enough.

¶ *Need help getting out of self-judgment? Revisit the "Let Judgment Go" meditation under "Rule" #8 in Section 4.*

You Are Good Enough

One of the places we're most likely to judge ourselves as not good enough is in our early drafts, especially if we're writing on the Muse Stream. The good news, sort of, is that first drafts are nearly never final drafts. Rather, your first draft is an opportunity to discover your story and to release it onto the page using the language of your heart, which is unlikely to be the perfectly executed language of your perfectly spelled, punctuated and grammared brain. That's okay. Allow it to be okay. Allow yourself to be okay with it. Don't judge yourself as not good enough because of it.

Later, you will revisit, review and revise this draft — using your heart-mind to bring it into closer alignment with your heart-vision.

Now, though, is the time to let your story speak to you and through you. Do that now and, whatever your critical mind might say, what you write will be good enough. It will be better than good enough. It will be yours.

It's easy to judge. It's easy to criticize. It's easy to say, "This isn't good enough," "This can never be good enough" or "I'm not good enough."

It's particularly easy with first drafts. It's just as easy with final drafts.

The truth is, you *are* good enough. If a story has chosen you to write it, then it is *your* story to write, which means you must be good enough to do it. Can you trust that?

Your writing, too, is good enough. It's good enough for this draft. In the next draft, you will make it better. The draft after that will be better still.

Leave judgment to judges who sit on the bench. Leave analysis to the analysts. Leave criticism to the critics. Your mission today is to write, to allow words to spill from you unhindered by judgment, unhampered by not-good-enoughs, uncrippled by comparisons.

You have judged yourself as wanting long enough. Now is the time to let self-judgment go and watch the Muse Stream flow.

• *See also "Say What?" in Section 12.*

Exploration

Ask yourself this question in your *Writer's Block Unblocked* journal but don't think about the answer. Let it emerge freely and honestly on the Muse Stream:

- Where in my life do I compare myself and/or my writing unfavorably to others? In what ways have those comparisons inhibited me or caused me to censor myself?

Try This

Take a break from this book to write on your story. Do it now. Write anything at all, as long as it relates in some way to the story you feel called to write. Write for 5 minutes or 50 but write, doing your best to leave judgment to the judges. Write. Now.

You don't yet know what your story is? Then open this book or any book to a random page, as you did with the first "Find Your Key" meditation in Section 3. Close your eyes, let your finger drop onto the page, and let the word or phrase your finger is touching be the key to this writing experience.

Alternatively, write on the Muse Stream from this phrase, "My story is..."

A Good Writer Is...

Of all the definitions of what makes a good writer, none that has any value is based on word counts. Nor are any based on numbers of manuscripts completed, books published or screenplays produced. However you choose to define "good writer" for yourself, avoid basing it on production quotas, or even on awards. Base it instead on how true you are to your vision, to your passion, to your Muse. Base it instead on how writing makes you feel...on how your writing makes others feel.

For me, a good writer is one who engages his or her readers, who immerses them in wondrous worlds that they are reluctant to leave, who writes with passion from a place of vision.

"But I write nonfiction," you argue. Then be passionate about your topic and write about it in a way that not only communicates that passion but injects it into every reader's mind and heart.

Share your passion openly, honestly and vulnerably. It's the first step in becoming not only a good writer but a great one.

7. Busted: Seven Common Writer's Block Myths

We're all creative.
RON HOWARD

Obligation is absolutely always the enemy of art.
JUDITH WESTON

The Myths

1. "I Have Writer's Block"

2. "Writer's Block Means I Have Nothing Creative, Original or Meaningful to Say"

3. "Writer's Block Means I'm Lazy"

4. "Writer's Block Means I'm Not Disciplined"

5. "Writer's Block Means I'm Not Really a Writer"

6. "Writer's Block Means I'm a Failure and Should Give Up"

7. "I Have Writer's Block"

1. "I Have Writer's Block"

Now that you have written (you *have* written, haven't you?), you can see that writer's block is a myth. Not only your writer's block. All writer's block. Writer's block does not exist, and you are not blocked. Yes, you may be feeling stuck. Or distracted. Or undisciplined. Or uncommitted. Or scared. Who hasn't in one moment or another?

Bust this myth yourself by erasing the phrase "I'm blocked" from your lexicon. As one of my coaching clients once pointed out, "If I redirected to my writing all the energy I now use to tell myself I'm blocked, I'd be writing like crazy!"

• *See also "Say What?" in Section 12.*

There Is No Writer's Block

There is no writer's block. There is only fear. When we stare at the blank page, the only marks on it the beads of saltwater sweat that drip from our stressed, frustrated brows, we are not experiencing a lack of talent. We are experiencing a fear so primal that it has probably been with us at least since childhood.

It has likely been with us since that first time someone judged us harshly or devalued us in some way. It happens all the time, and it happens, more often than not, from a misapplication of love than from love's absence.

Whatever the past created, the present can transform. Writing can transform your fear and pain into flow...into joy.

Why do you feel blocked? Because you fear to travel where your pen would guide you. Because you are afraid to surrender to the unknown gifts that await you. Because you are afraid to let go of all the controls that bind you to a place that feels safe but isn't.

Meet Annie. Annie was in her late fifties when she attended her first class of mine. Short, with close-cropped graying hair, she had a pixie's frame but lacked a pixie's spark.

"I want to write a memoir," she declared matter-of-factly when we introduced ourselves, each word measured, controlled. "But I have writer's block. I have had it for a decade."

She struggled with the early exercises, struggled against the controls she had placed on her self-expression. She feared going where her pen urged her to go, preferring to steer it in other, safer directions.

Yet when she finally surrendered to her pen and, perforce, to that pixie part of herself that was now, at last, finding expression, she had everyone in the class laughing so hard at the absurdities of her Earth Mother alter ego that we couldn't stop crying.

Annie, and that's not her real name, didn't have writer's block. She was afraid to embrace the part of herself that was light, funny, bizarre and uncontrollable. Once she did, her self-described block dissolved in a rush of daily writing — just for the pleasure of seeing where it would take her, just for the joy of surrender.

Try This

Write on the Muse Stream from this: "I follow my pen wherever it carries me. Today, it carries me to..." Or, "I follow the keys of my keyboard to wherever they direct my fingers. Today, they direct me to..."

After You've Written

Where did you end up? Was it difficult to let your pen or keyboard take charge...and stay in charge? What did you discover on the journey? Now, write about that.

2. "Writer's Block Means I Have Nothing Creative, Original or Meaningful to Say"

You can't not be creative. Free-flowing creativity is part of being human. It's coded into your genes, your cells, your DNA. Just because you aren't applying that creativity to the page today doesn't mean you're not creative. It simply means you're not writing today. You could be expressing your creativity in other ways — at your day job, in the kitchen, in the garden, with your camera, with your kids.

As Lajos Egri, author of *The Art of Creative Writing*, put it: "Without exception, everyone was born with creative ability." And film director Ron Howard echoes that in one of the quotes that opens this section: "We're all creative."

Your writing may not be flowing freely onto the page *in this moment*, but that has nothing to do with your creativity. You *are* creative.

Your Story, Your Way

Let's you and I and a dozen of our friends go to our favorite restaurant and order the same meal cooked the same way. When we're finished, let's each describe every component of the meal — how it looked, how it tasted, its texture, its aroma, its temperature, how it felt in the mouth, how its appearance blended with each of the other components, how it melded with the other tastes, textures and temperatures. Let's each say what the food reminded us of, what it evoked within us. Let's each describe the restaurant similarly. Then let's each tell a story about the food, the restaurant and our time together.

Although we will all have shared a common experience, we will each create of it a distinctive story, one that belongs only to its teller.

Or ask your siblings, parents or kids to write their version of a significant family event. Each version will be different from every other, and all will be different from yours.

In both instances, only your version of events will be infused with the singularity of your spirit, your outlook, your history and your heart. And infused as it will be with all those elements that distinguish you from others and link you to all humanity, your story will be as no other has been, is or ever could be. As such, how can it not be original? How can it not be creative?

What if you and a group of five hundred writers were to gaze up at an identical cloud? I guarantee that no two of you would see the same cloud. No two of you would write of the same cloud. Were you to give yourself permission to hear, trust and record the originality that flow from your heart at that precise moment, your interpretation would be unique...could only be unique. And your words would move, delight or offend the readers it needed to.

Other cloud-words would serve other readers. Others' heart-stories — about growing up or love or kids or war or betrayal or hatred or redemption — would touch whomever they need to touch. As would yours.

Your heart is different. It is touched by different things. It is moved by different expressions of the human emotions that move us all.

Your expression will touch others in ways you cannot imagine.

Once again, this is all predicated on your level of trust. Do you trust your truth enough to heed and record it? Do you trust yourself enough to go to the place of connection where you can hear it? These are your starting points. This is your life. Write it. Now.

Try This

Team up with a writing partner and write on the Muse Stream from the same keyword or key phrase. Agree on one from "Seventy Keys to Unlock Your Writing" (Section 3) or take turns choosing one. When you're done, share your writing (without judgment or self-criticism) and see how different your truth is from your partner's.

Expand the experience to a larger group with a Voice of the Muse Writers' Circle (see "Creative Connection" in Section 10).

Before sharing what you've written, read "Other Perspectives" (Section 10). Have your partner and fellow writer's group members read it too.

Creations of the Heart

You aren't writing because you're convinced that anything you might write (were you to give yourself permission to write) could only be derivative, self-indulgent or irrelevant. Probably all three. It certainly couldn't be original...or meaningful...or creative. It certainly couldn't have value...to you or to anyone.

You're wrong.

Every word that emerges in every writing session makes a unique contribution — be it a direct or an indirect one — to your creative life... to your life.

I'm not asking you to trust that your words will be perfect. I'm asking you to trust that each word will form part of a larger pattern that you will not recognize until you step back from it — later today, tomorrow, next week, next month or next year. Until you do, you are in no position to discern or determine anything, certainly not to judge anything.

You open a jigsaw puzzle box and toss its contents onto the floor. All you have is a collection of oddly shaped pieces that seem to go nowhere, connect with nothing — like your thoughts as you turn away from writing...like your words as you sit down to write...like the first draft of your story. Yet as you fit two puzzle pieces together, then ten, then thirty, a pattern slowly but inevitably emerges.

In your writing, too, a pattern will emerge.

Nothing of what you write is irrelevant or valueless. *Anything* that finds its way from heart to hand to page is relevant and significant. Anything and everything.

Trust that this is so...even as you cannot in this moment see or imagine how your words could ever string together to form a cogent and coherent whole. A creative whole.

This moment, now, as you read these words, may feel random and irrelevant. Yet this moment leads to the next and to the next. Then, from of all those moments, an hour forms, then a day, then a week, then a month, then a year, then a lifetime. And you discover in looking back that the moments that were the building blocks of that larger whole were integral to it, likely in ways you could not have known at the time. And that without them, there could have been no whole.

So trust. Trust that there is sense and wholeness within the words you carry in your heart. That sense and wholeness is hidden from you in this moment? That's why you must trust. That's why you must not only surrender to the mystery, but embrace it. Then, as you do, that elusive sense and wholeness will reveal itself it to you…in its time, not yours.

Are you still convinced that you have nothing of value to say? Nothing original? Nothing creative? If what you write comes from your place of authenticity, it cannot help but be creative and original. It cannot help but be meaningful…to you and to others.

3. "Writer's Block Means I'm Lazy"

There are many ways to nurture your creativity. Stepping away from writing can be one of them. It doesn't necessarily mean you're lazy...or blocked.

Sometimes the best gift we can give our creative process is time away from a *conscious* experience of it.

Time spent reading, walking or in meditation, for example, can be the perfect kick-start for a writing project. Time spent doing *anything* other than writing can be the ideal incubation environment for your creativity.

Have you ever had a great idea in the shower, at the gym or on a walk? That's because your mind is disengaged, and when your mind is disengaged, your Muse can engage directly with your heart, the true home of all passion-born creative projects.

¶ *See also Surefire Solution #3 in Section 8.*

The Miracle of the Seed

Like the seed that spends the first part of its life buried deep in the soil hidden from view, the seeds of your creations can also spend their early days, weeks, months or, sometimes, years germinating in the invisible realms of your unconscious.

It wasn't until I was forty and living in the fertile farm country of Nova Scotia's Annapolis Valley that I experienced my first real garden. Frankly, it wasn't much of a garden; more a postage-stamp vegetable patch. Yet, tiny as it was, it was abundant with carrots, cucumbers, spinach, beans, tomatoes...and lettuce.

I still remember feeling like the Jack of beanstalk fame as I ripped open that first packet of lettuce seeds and held those magic specks in my palm before sprinkling them into the soil I had prepared.

With a plant, the evidence of creation is always visible. But when you sow from seed, you operate in the realm of faith. Once that seed is covered over, all you can do is trust, water and wait.

My miracle wasn't as dramatic as Jack's. It was a pale green frond, delicate against the rusty soil. Yet that dainty lettuce leaf was as magical to me as any giant beanstalk.

Much of the magic resided in the effortlessness of the enterprise. My sole task had been to drop the seeds into the ground, trust the dark mystery of Mother Earth and wait. When the time was right for both of us, that lettuce leaf pushed through the moist earth and cried out, "Here I am!"

Writing can be as effortless. Buried in the dark mystery of our unconscious lie the seeds of books, short stories, screenplays, stage plays, songs, poems, essays and articles. They, like my lettuce seeds, dwell in a universe beyond our visual, tactile, mind-centered world. Like my lettuce leaf, they emerge in their time, when the season is right, when the moment is ripe.

You believe your inner place is devoid of ideas? Trust in the darkness and silence of the earth. Trust in the fertility of your creative process. Trust in the seeds that lie dormant beneath the surface.

Trust that what needs to emerge will emerge when you create the conditions for that emergence, when you allow yourself the same space and silence you allow your seeds. Trust in the seasons of your writing, and the words will break through.

Today, take time to nurture the seeds now germinating in the dark earth of your being. Sit in the silence without poking and prodding, without questioning and analyzing, without judging yourself as lazy or inadequate. Be the seed you are, and let the green shoots of your new growth develop and mature — into your awareness and onto the page.

Try This

Sometimes we're so busy doing, we never stop to be, to listen, to wait. Before you write today, give yourself 5, 10 or 20 minutes of nothingness, of silence. Sit in that silence as a seed sits in the soil. Breathe in the silence and breathe out your thoughts. Be in the stillness...breathe in the stillness...listen...and wait.

When you're ready to write, notice any differences in how you feel. Are you more, or less, anxious, fearful, ready? When you start writing, notice any differences in what you're writing, how you're writing...the quality of the experience...the quantity of the output.

After You've Written

What did the silence feel like, produce, open you to? Write about that too, today or another day, using any or all of these key phrases:

- In the silence, I...
- Through the silence, I...
- The silence guides me to...
- Because of the silence, I hear the still, small voice of my Muse. It...

4. "Writer's Block Means I'm Not Disciplined"

The primary definition of the word "discipline" in the *New Oxford American Dictionary* goes like this: "the practice of training people to obey rules or a code of behavior, using punishment to correct disobedience." Then there are the word's origins: from the Middle English, meaning "mortification by scourging oneself."

Punishment? Disobedience? Mortification? Scourging? That kind of discipline would shut any writer down.

It's time to take a Muse-centered look at discipline instead of the mind-centered one advanced by many writing books and teachers, who too often equate productivity and success with *Oxford*-like discipline. I refer to that kind of conventional discipline as "hard discipline" because of the ways it can feel harsh, strict and punishing and can leave you feeling less-than or not-good-enough. And it's toxic enough to build up the kind of blocks you have to come to these pages to deconstruct and dissolve.

Instead, let's deconstruct and dissolve that conventional approach by diving into the *heart* of discipline.

Into the Heart of Discipline

Traditional or "hard" discipline, the kind you generally read about, feels forced and rule-bound. Typically, it insists that you write at the same time and for the same length of time every day, and that you have the same writing goal for each session.

Hard discipline is disempowering and mistrustful because it suggests that you lack the commitment to write and the discernment to know when to write. Hard discipline also suggests that if you stray from this strict routine, you will never get anything done.

Don't get me wrong. There's nothing wrong with writing goals and routines. The problem arises when we serve the goal and routine, rather than having them serve us, when we are so married to them that they become more important than the writing, when the goal becomes a drag and the routine becomes a rut. (I'll talk more about writing routines in Surefire Solution #3 in Section 8.)

Heart discipline, on the other hand, is about discernment and intuition. Heart discipline is about passion and commitment. Heart discipline knows no set-in-stone rules, times or goals. Heart discipline is fluid and in-the-moment. Heart discipline places your Muse and story in the driver's seat of your creative enterprise.

Heart discipline is about discipleship. It's about you becoming a disciple to your Muse, to your work, to your vision. It is not about forcing a vision that is boundless in nature to hew to the constraints of a controlling mind or to be constricted by a "conventional wisdom" that is rarely wise.

Heart discipline says, "Trust." Trust that when you sit down, whenever you sit down, your Muse will be there for you, for your Muse is always present, always available and always ready. Trust that all you hear from your heart, including that it is either time to write or time to stop, is true. Trust that all the words that flow through you on a given day, be they five or five thousand, are the right ones.

Trust that should your Muse pull you out of a deep sleep at four in the morning, it is because four in the morning is the perfect time to write whatever is urging itself through you to be written.

Like intuition and discernment, trust is a practice. Practice listening to what's inside you. Practice listening to the voice of your Muse, the voice of your story and, where relevant, the voices of your characters, not to the judgmental, fear-based voices clamoring inside your head or to the disciplinary voices preaching at you from everywhere else.

Write what impassions, electrifies and enlivens you. Write the story you must write. Commit to that story with all your heart, and you will never lack the discipline to get it onto the page.

What if you have no passion for the story you're writing? Then you're writing the wrong one, and it's time to revisit "Rule" #2's "Is Your Write Idea the Right Idea for You?" (Section 4).

EXPLORATION

Ask yourself these questions in your *Writer's Block Unblocked* journal, but don't think about the answers. And don't feel you have to answer each question independently if that doesn't feel right.

Let your individual answers (or whatever single answer these questions trigger) emerge freely and honestly, writing them on the Muse Stream in a free-flowing, stream-of-consciousness way where appropriate. Let yourself be surprised by the answers.

- How have I approached discipline in the past? Was it "conventional" discipline? How did it feel? Did I ever find myself beating myself up for straying? How could I have approached that project differently? More self-lovingly?

- How can I apply heart discipline to the story I'm writing or feeling blocked from writing?

- How would the time spent with my story feel were my discipline less hard and more heart?

- How can I foster the trust that would free me from hard discipline and let my passion propel me forward? What can I do today, now, to foster that trust?

5. "Writer's Block Means I'm Not Really a Writer"

Most writers, including the famous ones, experience fallow periods. That doesn't make them non-writers. If you have written, you are a writer. If you're not writing right now but have not abandoned your passion and commitment, you are a writer. That you are here on this page, immersed in these words, proves that you are determined to write again...that you *will* write again. You *are* a writer!

Kafka Nearly Couldn't

It's early 1915 and Franz Kafka is in a creative slump. "The end of writing," he writes in his diary on January 20. "When will it take me up again?"

Things aren't looking much better nine days later: "Again tried to write, virtually useless."

By February 7, his writing has reached a "complete standstill."

Soon after, it's "another ten days and I have achieved nothing."

Although he's writing again by March 11, it's in unsatisfying fits and starts: "A page now and then is successful, but I can't keep it up, the next day I am powerless."

For all his creative and personal angst, Kafka continued writing until his death in 1924 from tuberculosis.

Today, Kafka is considered one of the giants of twentieth century literature and is best known for his novella *The Metamorphosis* and novels *The Trial* and *The Castle*. Even those who have never read his work are familiar with the term it inspired: Kafkaesque.

By the way, Franz Kafka had so little confidence in his work that he ordered all his diaries and unpublished work to be burned unread at his death. Fortunately for the world of great literature, his friend and literary executor, Max Brod, ignored those instructions.

Tolstoy's Complaint

Leo Tolstoy was so tormented while writing (or not writing) *Anna Karenina*, now thought to be one of the greatest novels of all time, that he considered suicide.

According to Bob Blaisdell, who chronicled Tolstoy's *Anna* journey in *Creating Anna Karenina: Tolstoy and the Birth of Literature's Most Enigmatic Heroine*, Tolstoy variously described the project as "sickening," "unbearably repulsive" and "disgusting and nasty." He stopped work on it multiple times during its creation, and Blaisdell estimates that Tolstoy avoided the manuscript for more than half the fifty-three months it took him to complete it.

Yet for all Tolstoy's despair-induced procrastination, Blaisdell suggests that it was only by persevering and so exhaustively documenting Anna's journey into madness and suicide that he survived his own emotional challenges.

Tolstoy continued writing after *Anna Karenina*'s publication, producing another novel (*Resurrection*), several novellas and countless short stories.

¶ *See also Section 11 ("On Rejection") for stories about writers who didn't let rejection stop them.*

6. "Writer's Block Means I'm a Failure and Should Give Up"

In a sense, neither success nor failure exists. No experience is ever that black-and-white. No experience is ever that absolute. Whatever the experience, however you perceive it and wherever it falls in that infinite array of intermediate tones between black and white, it has something to show us...something to teach us. It isn't a door slamming shut. It's a window opening into greater self-awareness.

Writer's block is no different. When the words won't come (or, more accurately, when you won't let them come), you have an opportunity to explore that reluctance. Of course, you can call yourself a failure and walk away. The more courageous path, though, is to stay with the experience and move through it to some sort of resolution.

Most writers who experience writer's block, including Franz Kafka and Leo Tolstoy, find that courage. You can too.

I Believe in You

It's easy to feel discouraged and disheartened, to feel defeated and destroyed. It's easy to shout "I'm done" and give up.

Don't do it.

Whatever its source, don't yield to the despair. Whatever has sparked it, don't give in to the hopelessness. Whatever has triggered it, don't give in to the desperation and depression.

Feel what you feel, always. But don't let yourself stop there. Don't let yourself get stuck there. Don't let yourself be paralyzed into inaction.

Whoever you are, whatever your story, you have done so much, come so far. It doesn't always feel that way, but it's true.

Don't squander all you have accomplished and achieved by stopping now. Don't give up on your dreams. Don't give up on your passion. Don't give up on your story...on your stories. Don't give up on yourself.

I believe in you.

Never Give Up!

In my novel *Sara's Year*, two of the characters enter their teen years with powerful dreams and ambitions. One yearns to be a writer; the other, an artist.

By the time they reach their early twenties, however, both dreams have been abandoned. Life has a way of getting in the way, when we let it...and both those women do.

The good news for one of the two is that, ultimately, she not only revives a dream that she believed to have been lost for good, she finds a way to dive into it and live it...with monumental success.

It wasn't too late for Sara to live her dream of being a writer, and it's never too late for you to live yours.

It's never too late to rekindle the hope that has shriveled into hopelessness. And it's never too early to give up on the idea of giving up.

"I Am a Writer. Period."

It's August 2013, a few weeks before my fifty-ninth birthday, and I have just completed a first draft of a stage-musical adaptation of *The SunQuest*, third story in my *Legend of Q'ntana* fantasy series. I have been at this nonstop for eight weeks now. I began by adapting *The MoonQuest*, the first story, and continued straight through with *The StarQuest* and *The SunQuest*. I'm beyond burnt out.

For more than twenty-five years, I have treated writing as a spiritual pursuit, writing from the deepest inner places I have been able to access. It's also what I've taught. But on this day, I feel as though I have sacrificed too much for too little: My book sales are poor, my coaching income is negligible, I no longer have a home or car of my own and the emotional pain of digging so deep has grown unbearable.

On this day, I declare to my closest friends that I'm on strike. "If I'm going to return to writing," I insist, "something has to shift. Otherwise, I'm giving it up. The work is much too hard for so pitiful a payoff."

My friends, some of whom are writers themselves, make sympathetic noises. I'm certain that they don't doubt my sincerity, but I suspect they doubt my determination.

"Let them doubt," I mutter as I settle into a diet of Netflix and murder mysteries. "If nothing changes, I'm not going back."

I make one modest concession: I commit to editing and posting the "prestrike" interview I conducted with *New York Times* bestselling mystery author J.A. Jance.

About thirty minutes into our recorded conversation, as we're chatting about craft, I tell Jance how much I love that she never outlines her books because I don't either.

"I have to sort of step out with faith," she says, "that if I can write the first sentence of the book, I can eventually get to the end of it."

"Shit," I exclaim to the recording. The moment Jance talks about the faith that carries her from her first sentence to her last, I know that my strike is over. My creative and spiritual lives have always been inextricably linked, and both have been built on a solid foundation of spiritual faith.

As Jance's words echo in my heart and mind, I realize that if the deepest part of me has determined that I am a writer and that my writing (and all that derives from it) is the most important part of my being, I can't walk away from it. I can't give up. I can't abandon my faith and I can't stop surrendering to it.

I am a writer. Period.

¶ *See also "Feeling Rejected? Don't Be Dejected" in Section 11 and "Living the Creative Life" in Section 13.*

7. "I Have Writer's Block"

Remember Writer's Myth #1 from Section 6 and Writer's Block Myth #1 from this section? *Writer's block does not exist, and you are not blocked.*

If writer's block doesn't exist, then not one of these myths matters. Nothing matters but that you're writing.

You aren't? Your page is still blank? It's probably time for a Muse Stream refresher. Revisit "Flowing Forward" (Section 2) for the basics, then write *anything* on the Muse Stream, using one of the exercises in "The Muse Stream and You" (Section 3) or from anywhere else in the book. Once you've done that, burst from the confines of your cocoon with "The Butterfly" meditation in the next chapter.

The Butterfly
A Guided Meditation

Allow at least 20 minutes to complete this meditation and for the writing that flows from it.

My studio recording of this meditation is available for download or streaming as part "The Voice of the Muse Companion: Guided Meditations for Writers." See "Guided Meditations" in Section 1 ("Getting Started") to find out how to access the recording, as well as for tips on how best to use this book's meditations.

Close your eyes. Breathe in deeply, fully. Allow your shoulders to drop, then drop some more. And some more. Allow yourself to relax. Fully.

From that place of calm, let your breath transport you into the realm of imagination, the realm of creativity, the realm of vision.

See yourself now in another form, another body. A caterpillar's body.

You're a caterpillar, enfolded in a cocoon. Like a blanket-bundled infant or your blanket-bundled sleep-in self, you're enveloped in the divine caress of in-between time.

In this moment, you're safe. Safe in the all-embracing darkness. Secure in the womb of creation, transformation, rebirth.

Creation. Transformation. Rebirth.

Feel that transformation within you. Feel your shape begin to shift. Feel your body lighten and wings begin to form.

Feel the nascent emergence of color, translucence, delicacy.

Now, feel the pressure of your wings as, pressed between your body and the walls of the cocoon, they push and spread, push and spread. Push and spread.

Such delicate wings, yet so strong.

So strong.

Such a delicate body, yet so strong.

So strong.

So awake. So determined. So ready.

What was once a sanctuary is now stifling. What once held you in safety now presses against you, holds you down. Holds you back.

Thank the cocoon and the caterpillar you were for letting you sleep, for keeping you safe, for holding you secure. Thank them and release them from the need to do so any longer.

Now it's time to awaken.

Now it's time to fly.

Now it's time to be a creature of earth and sky. Of sky and earth.

Now it's time to travel great distances, to soar to great heights, to stretch the limits of the possible. To enter into the realm of the improbable, the realm of the impossible.

Feel the walls of your cocoon give way. Feel your wings spread as they push and push and push some more.

It's hard work, at times, to push free of the barriers we have created for ourselves. But we always have the strength. We always have the will. We always have the power.

All we need to do is acknowledge our strength, surrender to our highest imperative, and allow our power to have its way with us.

It's time to surrender. To the butterfly you are. To the creator you are. To the free-flowing, free-flying being you are.

So do it.

Push one last time with those wings that seem so delicate but carry the strength and will of the universe. Push one last time and feel the walls of your cocoon break apart.

Now, spread your wings to the fullness of their span and fly free.

Fly free.

Fly *free.*

Now.

You may feel tentative, uncertain. Shaky. That's normal. These are new wings, new experiences, new expressions. Allow the uncertainty, knowing that with each flight you *will* become more certain, more practiced, more adept.

Fly for as long as you like. Explore your new world from this new perspective. Take your time. And when you're ready to light down again — on a flower petal, on a leaf or on a blank sheet of paper that has fluttered to earth — open your eyes and write about your experiences, your feelings, your journey.

Write about them as the caterpillar-turned-butterfly, describing your transformation, your liberation, your flight.

And write about them as the writer you are, now free of one more barrier to your freest, fullest expression.

Try This

Consider making some unique variation of "I can do it" or "I am a writer" or "I make my own rules" or "I write with ease" or "I am a butterfly" as the username or password for a frequently used login. Repeatedly typing a statement like that will help reinforce it for you.

8. Get Unblocked! Seven Surefire Solutions

> Writers have a little holy light within, like a pilot light, which fear is always blowing out.
> CYNTHIA OZICK

> I won't try to convince you that I've never plotted any more than I'd try to convince you that I've never told a lie, but I do both as infrequently as possible. I distrust plot...
> STEPHEN KING

Seven Surefire Solutions

1. Say *No* to Fear

2. Abandon Control

3. Rethink Your Routines

4. Strive for Excellence, Not Perfection

5. Learn to Tell the Write Time

6. Rekindle Your Passion

7. Say *Yes* to You

1. Say "No" to Fear

Fear will always stop us from moving forward in our writing, if we let it. Fear of success. Fear of failure. Fear of judgment. Fear of criticism. Fear of ridicule. Fear of love. Fear of lack. Fear of shame. Fear of praise. Fear of what we might reveal — to ourselves or to others. Fear of consequences we can imagine. Fear of consequences we dare not imagine. Fears we can't identify. Fears we don't even know we have.

The only antidote is to keep writing — through the fear, whatever it is. Past the fear, however it shows up.

Your fears — and all your emotions — can be the most powerful components of your writing. Remember "Rule" #7? Go for the jugular. *Your* jugular.

Don't run from your fears. Write them. Write them on the Muse Stream. Write them in your journal. Write them into your stories and characters. Write them onto the page and out of you.

Write the Fear

Our fears lie in layers within us. Strip away one layer, resolve it, and in time another will reveal itself.

You have dissolved many layers to reach this point on your creative path. You have resolved much, and yet...

What is it you still fear? Discover it by writing it. Acknowledge it. Then let it go.

It is both the writing and the releasing that allow the true writing to emerge. You may write pages and pages and pages of fear before you reach the place of no-fear, the place of flow, the place of freedom, the place where your story resides.

What emerges when you get there may surprise you. Let it.

What is it you fear? Which word do you fear placing before you today? Which word do you fear placing in front of the world? Do you dare write the first letter? The second?

What do you still fear? Write the question and let the answer write itself. Let the answers write themselves.

Of all those, which is the core or root fear? Or is the core another fear altogether? Again, write the question and let the answer reveal itself to you on the Muse Stream.

What is your payoff for that fear, those fears? In other words, what do you gain from that fear? How does it act as an incentive? What dividends does it yield in your life?

Once again, write the question and let your pen or fingers on the keyboard spell out the answer.

Are you surprised by the answer? Sit with it for a few minutes before reading on.

Now, using the payoff as your keyword or key phrase, write on the Muse Stream for fifteen or twenty minutes — longer, if that's what will free you to feel complete — and see what emerges.

When you're done, set your writing aside and breathe deeply as you inhale your freedom from another fear, as you exhale another block.

What was it you feared? Whatever it was no longer matters. You have released it onto the page, given it permission to breathe and watched its power over you melt away on that breath.

You are free now. Free to write. Free to breathe. Free to be.

Making Friends with Your Inner Critic

There's a scene in *Star Trek: The Next Generation* where Jean-Luc Picard is presented with a sculpture of a humanoid. When he lifts off the removable top of the art piece, more than a dozen identical beings are nested inside it.

Like that sculpture, we carry within us many facets and aspects that make up the greater whole we view as Self.

If you're feeling stuck in your writing, it can be helpful to identify and connect with that part of you that wants to block your forward movement.

How? It isn't as hard as it might sound. First, let me tell you a story…

It's about a dream of mine from many years ago. A nightmare. In it,

I'm trying to walk out of an underground parking garage, but the uniformed attendant refuses to let me pass out onto the street.

I argue. He argues back.

I shout. He shouts back.

Everything I say or do is met with unyielding resistance.

I'm stuck, and I wake up nauseous and sweating.

A few days later, I decide to try to reproduce the dream in meditation to see if I can alter the outcome. Using the inner or meditative dialogue technique I describe in Section 4, I call the surly guard back into my consciousness. Once again, I attempt to leave. Once again, he refuses me passage. This time, however, instead of arguing with him, I calmly ask him why.

As we dialogue back and forth, he reveals that his job is to protect me. "If I let you leave," he argues, "I'll be out of work."

For a moment, I'm startled by the disclosure. Then, from some deep well of inner wisdom, I reassure him that I still need his protection, but in new ways.

Relieved, he agrees to learn to act more as a filter than a block. When we're done, we embrace, and I stride past him and out into the sunlight, knowing that I have turned a barrier to my forward movement into a willing and eager helper.

Now It's Your Turn...

Often, even if at an unconscious level, we are invested in whatever is holding us back. Sometimes, it's a fear of success that can be even more debilitating than a fear of failure. Sometimes, we're afraid that whatever we write will change us so radically that it will render us unrecognizable, as much to ourselves as to others. How are you invested in your inability to move forward with your writing?

Get comfortable, close your eyes, breathe into a relaxed meditative state and focus on that question — not from your mind but from your heart. Then open your eyes and write on the Muse Stream from this key phrase, "My writer's block helps me to..."

Write until you feel complete, then keep writing for a further fifteen or twenty minutes to go deeper.

Were you surprised? Whatever it was that emerged will assist you in the next chapter, as you "Talk to Your Block."

Talk to Your Block

Use this do-it-yourself version of the exercise or, if you prefer a more guided approach, the "Making Friends with Your Inner Critic" meditation that follows in the next chapter.

As I mentioned in the previous chapter, we are made up of many, sometimes conflicting facets and aspects. If you are feeling creatively stifled, at least one of them is blocking you. And it's probably scared, as mine was.

As you did in your first Muse Stream exercises, use your breath to get into a relaxed, meditative space. If you are still feeling tense, run slowly up through your body — from your toes to the top of your head — breathing consciously into any areas that feel especially stressed.

Then, gently and with love, invite a blocked part of yourself to sit down with you.

You can do this silently with your eyes closed, or you can write the conversation down as it's happening, allowing the answers to flow to you on the Muse Stream. Whichever method you choose, do your best to not think about what's going on, to remain compassionate and free of judgment and to ask all your questions without emotional charge.

Start by asking that part of you to identify itself and to explain why it is holding you back from writing or from working on a particular project.

This is not about eliminating, expelling or killing off any part of you. That would be an unhealthy and self-destructive way of going about this. Rather, it's about finding out what sparked your apparent block.

Perhaps, as with my parking attendant, that part of you is trying to protect the rest of you from something. Or perhaps it has reasons unique to your situation. Whatever is revealed to you through this process, begin by thanking that part of you for having protected you in the past and by reassuring it that it is still necessary in your life, in new ways.

From there, invite it to explore with you how motivation might be renewed and forward motion reignited. Ask it to now act as more of a filter than a block. Ask for its help, but remember to keep the powerful, fearless part of you lovingly in charge of the process.

Use these and/or your own questions and allow the answers to come naturally, whether on the page or in your mind's eye. Don't force the answers. Don't judge or censor. Remember to breathe. If you need help, revisit the Muse Stream tips in Section 2.

- Who are you? Do you have a name?
- Why don't you want me to write? / Why don't you want me to write on [name of project]?
- What are you afraid of?
- What can I do to reassure you? What would make you feel safer?
- How can I retrain you? How can you become less blocking and more discerning? How can you become less of a wall and more of a filter? Less a solid door and more a screen door?

If you don't get all the answers you seek in a single session, rejoin the conversation another day, and another, if necessary.

If you still feel blocked after having a meditative dialogue with one part of yourself, call in another and repeat the experience.

This same exercise can also be valuable in addressing blocks in your personal or professional life.

Making Friends with Your Inner Critic
A Guided Meditation

Allow at least 30 minutes to complete this meditation and for the writing that flows from it.

My studio recording of this meditation is available for download or streaming as part "The Voice of the Muse Companion: Guided Meditations for Writers," where it's titled "Taming Your Critic." See "Guided Meditations" in Section 1 ("Getting Started") to find out how to access the recording, as well as for tips on how best to use this book's meditations.

Sit or lie down in a comfortable position. Close your eyes and take a few deep breaths. Let yourself relax. Feel yourself relax on your breath.

Now, let your shoulders drop...and drop some more. And some more. And some more. Breathe deeply and fully, feeling the breath fill not only your lungs and abdomen, but your entire body — from head to toes and back.

And again.

And again.

Feel the breath cleanse you. Feel it dissolve your fears, your anxiety, your stress. Feel it strengthen you, empower you. Feel it protect you, keep you safe. Feel it open your heart. Feel it open your mind.

There have been times in your life when you have been criticized, times in your life when you have been judged. Of course there have. We have all had those experiences. As children. As adolescents. As adults.

Sometimes, the experience rolled off us painlessly. Sometimes, it felt excruciatingly cruel. Sometimes, we forged ahead in spite of it. Sometimes, it shut us down.

It's all normal, all perfect, all part of the human experience. And as with all human experience, we can choose how to react or respond, we can choose how each instance will affect us.

Don't judge how you have reacted or responded in the past. Just be aware and keep breathing. Fully. Deeply. Allow your breath to once again dissolve any stress or anxiety triggered by unpleasant memories.

Know that you are safe. Protected.

Free from harm of any sort.

From that place of relaxed breathing, from that place of safety, call into your mind, heart and/or consciousness your harshest critic. Perhaps it's someone in your past or present life. A teacher. A parent. A sibling. Another relative. A friend. A school or neighborhood bully. A boss, professional colleague or coworker.

Feel whatever charge you feel around this individual, and breathe. Feel whatever charge you feel around this individual and let that feeling dissolve on your breath.

Now, let that critic transform into some kind of image, something that represents that critic, that stands in for that critic. A symbol. A metaphor. Perhaps it's an animal. Perhaps it's a color or shape. Perhaps it's a snake or serpent. Perhaps it's another human form or another type of form altogether. Or perhaps it doesn't change form at all.

Let it be what it is and know that however it shows up is perfect for you in this moment. Regardless of how it shows up, see it not as an external critic but as an internalized aspect of you, ready to engage with you.

Whatever it is, whoever it is, however it is, greet it and begin a dialogue with it. Have a conversation with it. Engage with it.

Write this dialogue as it occurs, or let it emerge silently in your heart.

In the first part of your conversation, ask your critic why it judged you so cruelly, what provoked its behavior, what it was afraid of.

If this is an ongoing situation, frame your questions in the present tense.

Listen with an open heart. Respond with an open heart. Allow compassion. Allow understanding. Allow forgiveness. Allow love.

Give yourself thirty seconds of clock time for this part of the experience. Or pause the meditation until you are ready to continue.

Be aware that if you are experiencing judgment, you are probably expressing judgment somewhere in your life. Have compassion for yourself for *your* judgments. Be understanding. Be forgiving. Be loving. Be open. Be respectful. Toward yourself.

Commit as well to directing those same attitudes toward others, toward anyone you are tempted to criticize harshly.

Now, as you return to the conversation with your critic, ask it how the two of you can work together from this moment forward to bring your work, your writing and your life to its fullest, most magnificent potential.

Converse. Discuss. Negotiate. Dialogue. Engage. Silently or in writing.

Again, be loving and compassionate. Be understanding and forgiving. Be respectful. Be open.

Allow another thirty seconds of clock time for this part of the experience. Or, again, pause the meditation until you're ready to continue.

Now it's time to bring your encounter to a close. Thank this aspect of yourself for its assistance, for its openness, for its willingness to transform. And commit to this new partnership. Commit, too, to the spirit of cooperation the two of you have now forged in love and mutual respect.

When you're done, write of your experiences and discoveries. Use all your senses to paint a picture in words of your new awareness and your renewed creative power.

When you're finished writing, remember to read your words from a place of love, openness and non-judgment. Remember, too, your commitment to partnership and cooperation.

Risky Writing

Creative expression is about risk-taking. It's about boarding *Star Trek*'s Starship *Enterprise*, taking off for parts unknown and journeying to places where no one before has dared to go.

When you do that, chances are that not everyone is going to like what you have written. Chances are that someone will hate what you have written. It's even possible that someone will hate you for what you have written.

It's all right to offend people, to push people's buttons, to take them up to that ledge on which we, as artists, live...and then to give them a gentle nudge. Art is about pushing boundaries — yours as well as those of others. It's about forcing people (including the artist) out of their comfort zone and inciting them to reexamine their beliefs and rediscover who they think they are. Sometimes, it's about getting people mad at you. Sometimes, it's good to get people mad at you — for them and for you.

"You've got to go out on a limb," humorist Will Rogers is reputed to have said, "because that's where the fruit is."

Where are you going out on a limb and taking risks with your writing? Where are you staying on the ground and clinging to the tree trunk to play it safe?

Where are you willing to get people riled up? Where are you holding yourself back for fear of being shamed, ridiculed or attacked?

Commit today to taking more risks, to going out on a limb. Commit today to letting yourself be judged...and letting it be okay.

Exploration I

Ask yourself these questions in your *Writer's Block Unblocked* journal, but don't think about the answers. Let them emerge freely and honestly on the Muse Stream. Let yourself be surprised by the answers.

- How can I be more daring in my life today?
- How can I blaze new trails and go where no one has dared to go — in my writing and in my life?

Exploration II

Close your eyes for a minute, take a deep breath, and connect with one risk, even a tiny one, that you're prepared to take to become the writer you dream of being...a writer who's true to your heart, your soul and your passion. Connect with that risk and know that, in faith, nothing is truly a risk. Connect with it and commit to taking it. Now.

¶ *See also "Heartful Acts of Revolution," Section 12.*

Say "No" to Shame

Author and poet Dorothy Allison writes frankly about her working-class background and about the poverty and relentless sexual abuse of her childhood.

"Until I started pushing on my own fears, telling the stories that were hardest for me, writing about exactly the things I was most afraid of and unsure about, I wasn't writing worth a damn," she has said.

Sharing her vulnerabilities with the world has earned Allison both praise and censure. A three-time winner of the Lambda Literary Award and a National Book Award finalist, she outraged mainstream feminists with her first book, the poetry collection *The Women Who Hate Me*. And her novel *Bastard Out of Carolina* has been banned nearly as often as it has been lauded.

"I was born in 1949," she said in a 2012 interview, "and by the time I was ten, I figured out that...I could either be provocative and declamatory, or shy, retiring and scared. And ashamed. I couldn't do much about scared; I was always going to be scared. But I could damn well fight off shame."

EXPLORATION

Do you know what you're most ashamed of? In your writing? In your life? Sometimes, we're clear on the source of our greatest shame. Frequently, though, it lies beneath the surface of our conscious awareness, generally because we're too frightened or embarrassed to acknowledge it. This lack of awareness inevitably gets in the way of creating to our fullest potential...of living to our fullest potential.

For the first part of this exploration, write on the Muse Stream from the phrase "I'm most ashamed of..." Don't stop with a surface shame; keep writing to go deeper. No one ever has to see this writing, so do your best to follow the Muse Stream wherever it takes you, however uncomfortable the journey and/or destination.

For the second part of this exploration, be like Dorothy Allison and write about the shame. Not necessarily for public consumption, but to help work its emotional toxins out of your system. Tell the story of the shame's origins or describe a later time when the shame played out in your life. To ensure that you don't hold back or censor yourself, write it on the Muse Stream.

AFTER YOU'VE WRITTEN

Were you surprised by what emerged? Was it difficult to surrender into the Muse Stream? Don't read over what you've written right away, unless you can do it from a place of compassion and non-judgment. If you need help getting to that place, revisit the "Let Judgment Go" meditation in Section 4. Regardless, congratulate yourself for your courage and for, like Dorothy Allison, telling one of the stories that was hardest for you. In doing so, you busted through a major blockage! Be sure to include this accomplishment in your Success Diary (Section 4).

2. Abandon Control

When we assume that we are in charge of our story, that it has to look or sound a specific way, conform to a particular genre or format, or match a certain outcome or expectation, we are nearly guaranteed to get stuck.

Your story has its own imperative and its own wisdom. You override those at your peril.

Abandon control. Let your story express itself. Let your characters tell you their story. Let your Muse have its way with you. Let the words spill out of you — the words your story needs, not the words you think it needs. Not the words you think you need. Remember "Rule" #9 and strip off those straitjackets.

It's Time to Let Go

Imagine a sparrow trying to take off while gripping a rabbit in its claws. Even if it could get off the ground, how high do you think it would rise?

Imagine yourself holding on to a large, heavy crate. Even were you able to stumble forward, how far do you think you would manage to walk?

That rabbit and crate are like the people, places, things, situations, concerns and emotions we cling to because we clutch at the illusion of safety and security they represent, because we won't trust our heart to keep us safe...because we won't trust the voice of our Muse to lead the way.

Whatever form they take, these are the blocks that hinder the free flow of our writing, that prevent us from expressing our full creative potential...our full life potential.

It's time to unclench. It's time to release. It's time to let go.

Whose Story Is It?

Some years back, I was listening to a guest speaker — let's call him Tom — at a writer's group. He was talking about characters.

"In the first half of your story," he counseled, "let your characters do what they want. But when you get to the second half, you've got to rein them in."

Tom was adamant, and it took all my self-control to rein myself in… not because of the first half of his statement, but because of the second.

I was reminded of that story some months later when I began working with Karen, then a new coaching client. Karen had written a powerful memoir, so powerful that it had been nominated for a literary award. Now, a fictional character had accosted her in a misty Celtic glen and was insisting she write his story.

"I've never written a novel," she moaned. "I don't know how!"

"You don't have to know how," I replied. "All you have to do is write his memoir."

You see, whatever fictional story we're telling — be it a novel, short story, stage play or screenplay — we're writing someone's story.

Let me say that again: What we are doing is writing *their* story. And what we often discover in our first draft is not only what that story is, but who that character is…who all the characters are who make up that world.

Tom's point was that we spend the first half of our story discovering who the character is. From there, we spend the rest of the story ensuring that our character doesn't stray from that portrait.

My point is that we may only know the truth of who that character is and what he or she is about by writing through to the end. Why stifle the creative process just when we have finally surrendered to the story's unfoldment? Why limit ourselves and our characters by insisting that at a certain point in the draft, character and story are fixed for all time?

Pushing your characters to do or be something that's untrue to their nature is an invitation to writer's block. At least that's what novelist and short story writer Anne Tyler has found. Tyler has written that when she hits what she calls a "real block," it's "usually because I've taken a wrong turn — said something false or made a character do what he doesn't want to do." Anne Tyler, by the way, isn't any ordinary writer.

She's a Pulitzer Prize winner for her novel *Breathing Lessons*. Two of her other novels (she's written two dozen) were Pulitzer Prize finalists, and two others were Man Booker Prize finalists.

When I was working on my first draft of *The StarQuest*, I had a fairly clear idea of how one of my antagonists would meet her downfall in the closing scenes. At least, I thought I did…

Then, on my final day's work on that initial draft, as I was letting the penultimate scene write itself, something unanticipated happened: Instead of the ugly death I was expecting for her, this villain had a jaw-droppingly different experience, one that left me stunned and confused.

In that moment, I had two choices: I could follow Tom's advice and refuse my villain her experience, or I could give in to the higher imperative of both the character and the story and surrender to the magic. I chose the latter, not only because I believe my stories and their characters are smarter than I am, but because this character's unexpected transformation supported what I had begun to recognize as one of the story's central themes, and it achieved it in ways that I would have been hard-pressed to consciously manufacture.

In the "'Rules' for Creating Compelling Characters" that I share in my "Free Your Characters, Free Your Story!" workshops, "Rule" #11 reads "Respect Revolution: How did John become Jane? And why is she suddenly the villain?"

Often, characters in our stories want to undergo revolutionary changes through the course of that first draft. Too often, we follow Tom's advice and refuse them that freedom.

My view is that our job as Writer God is to give our characters absolute freedom through the entire first draft of our story…and, sometimes, beyond.

Unlike Tom, I say: Let your characters be as inconsistent and mercurial as they want to be. Let them veer off in radically different directions partway, if that is what they choose. Let your villains become heroes and your heroes become villains. Let them change names, physical characteristics, motivations and story-significance. Let them change gender. Let them change species.

Only by allowing them that unconditional freedom in your first draft can you learn who they truly are and can you be true to their story. After all, it's their story you're telling.

Let your first draft be that imperfect journey of discovery: of your characters and of their story. Through that journey, you will grow into your story and its characters.

You might, as I did in *The StarQuest*, only discover something of major significance about an important character on the final page of the draft. That's okay. Use your next draft to bring consistency to the characters you now know more fully.

Remember whose story you're telling…and get out of the way.

Exploration

Ask yourself these questions in your *Writer's Block Unblocked* journal, but don't think about the answers. And don't feel you have to answer each question independently if that doesn't feel right.

Let your individual answers (or whatever single answer these questions trigger) emerge freely and honestly, writing them on the Muse Stream in a free-flowing, stream-of-consciousness way where appropriate. Let yourself be surprised by the answers.

- How can I better trust my characters and their stories to reveal themselves to me?
- Can I free my characters and their stories to be what they are, not what I think they should be?
- How can I let myself be surprised — by my characters and by their stories?
- How can I let myself be surprised — as much by the story I'm living as by the story I'm writing?
- How can I better surrender to the magic out of which all creativity is birthed?

Embrace the Chaos

"When people see the nice books with the nice white pages and the nice black writing," Margaret Atwood has said, "what they don't see is the chaos and the complete frenzy and general shambles that the work comes out of."

Writing is an act of creating something out of nothing. It's the process of converting primordial sludge into art. It's the Godlike feat of shaping words and worlds out of a formless void. And if Genesis makes throwing together a finished world in six days look easy, it's probably because it edited out the frenzied bits that Atwood talks about.

In fiction, characters change their names, ages and genders at will, transforming themselves from protagonists to antagonists or from bit players to leads for reasons known only to them. Plots pretzel around and in on themselves multiple times over, leading you, the writer, on a bewildering journey that only begins to make sense once it has ended.

In nonfiction, premises, themes and conclusions pull you into a demented square dance, switching partners and direction on you with mind-twisting frequency.

In both, first chapters become final chapters, final chapters get edited out, restored and edited out again, and middle bits get rewritten until they are unrecognizable, only to become books of their own.

It wasn't until I was halfway through my first draft of *The SunQuest*, for example, that I discovered why I had felt the need to excise large chunks of *The StarQuest* after I completed its seriously chaotic first draft. Turned out I had written those scenes for the wrong story; they belonged in *The SunQuest*. (Moral: Keep your outtakes.)

Creation is messy work. From first draft to last, it's anything but orderly and any attempts to control it will, at best, stifle your story's best expression. At worst, it will block you.

Trust the disorderly process that is at the root of all creative acts. Free your characters. Free your plots. Free your narrative. Free your arguments and ideas. Embrace the chaos.

EXPLORATION

Ask yourself these questions and don't think about the answers. Let them emerge freely and honestly...on the Muse Stream, where appropriate. Let yourself be surprised by the answers.

- In general, how well do I handle chaos in my creative pursuits?
- How can I flow more easily with Margaret Atwood's "complete frenzy and general shambles" and embrace the chaos inherent in all creative acts?

Trickster Tales

The Trickster is a mythological and archetypal figure that dupes its victims into doing its bidding. Mischievous by nature, it will lie unashamedly and break any rule to get its way.

In myth, think leprechauns (Ireland), coyotes (U.S. Southwest), the Greek god Dionysus and the Hawaiian/Polynesian demigod Maui. In literature and popular culture, think Puck in *A Midsummer Night's Dream*, *King Lear*'s Fool (along with every court jester ever conceived), Q in *Star Trek: The Next Generation*, Bart Simpson, the Pink Panther and Bugs Bunny.

Your story and Muse are also tricksters. As you craft the story you think you are writing, they will often trick you into writing something you never expected to write, something you never thought you wanted to write, something, perhaps, that is uncomfortable to write.

This is good.

Curse, mutter and resist if you must. Then give in. Your story will always take you not only to the place of creative magic, awe and wonder, but to the place where its ideal expression resides…if you abandon control and let it.

Let it.

EXPLORATION

Ask yourself these questions in your *Writer's Block Unblocked* journal, but don't think about the answers. And don't feel you have to answer each question independently if that doesn't feel right.

Let your individual answers (or whatever single answer these questions trigger) emerge freely and honestly, writing them on the Muse Stream in a free-flowing, stream-of-consciousness way where appropriate. Let yourself be surprised by the answers.

- Where have my stories surprised me? Shocked me? Scared me? Tricked me?

- Where is my current story propelling me out of my comfort zone? Am I resisting? How?

- What unexpected and/or disturbing things am I discovering through my writing? About my story? About myself?

It's All in Order...Even When It Isn't

Like movies, which are rarely filmed in sequence, your first (or second or third) draft may not write itself in final story order. *Writer's Block Unblocked* certainly didn't.

In this as in all aspects of your writing enterprise, let the bits and pieces of your story come as they come...and write them that way, knowing that your story's innate wisdom will determine the appropriate order when the time is right.

Writing that way may feel scattered and uncontrolled. But as I've noted throughout these pages, insisting that your story be written a certain way or forcing it into a certain direction is a surefire path to writer's block.

Sometimes, writing a scene or chapter out of sequence — intentionally or not — can reveal to you aspects of your story's theme, premise or, in fiction, characters that you might otherwise have overlooked or have taken longer to discover. Sometimes, too, postponing a challenging part of your story can help keep you writing when you hit a roadblock.

Follow the Muse Stream where it takes you, and don't second-guess your story-directed creative journey. Let your story's natural order emerge organically, not through any act of will on your part.

Feeling Stuck? Try This...

Move on to another scene, chapter, section or sequence. Return to this one in an hour, in a day or in a few days — whenever you feel ready or after you have carried out the necessary research, if a research-deficit is what has stopped you. Is it an emotionally challenging segment that's holding you back? Try journaling about your resistance, or revisit your vision statement.

3. Rethink Your Routines

Whether it's our first-thing-in-the-morning regimen, the regular route we take to work or where we walk our dog, we human beings cherish our routines. It's no different with our creative life, where we often prefer a set writing time and place and, if we write longhand, the same favorite pen and notebook.

Rituals and routines, however, can turn into ruts. What worked yesterday may not work today...or ever again. Remember "Rule" #1?

If you're feeling stuck, you may well be stuck — in a pattern that isn't working for you anymore. Maybe it's time to break away from some of those old patterns and experiment with new ones. Write in the morning instead of the afternoon, longhand instead of on the computer, in a café instead of at home.

Find the writing routine that works for you today, and be open to changing it tomorrow.

TRY THIS

What can you do *today* to break the patterns that are keeping you rutted in routine, in your writing or in your life?

If you commute regularly to work, alter your route or mode of transport or both. Is there someplace you regularly shop? Shop somewhere else instead, maybe in a different part of town. Do you have a regular coffee hangout? Try somewhere new, perhaps in a neighborhood you don't know, and change your regular drink for something you've never tried before.

What about your writing routines? Read on for seven surefire ways to rethink them.

Seven Surefire Ways to Rethink Your Writing Routines

In the decade before *The MoonQuest* urged itself on me, I was a freelance writer and editor, working on magazines and with universities, government agencies and businesses to fulfill their institutional needs. Most days, I sat at my home-office desk and wrote or edited articles, brochures, reports, speeches and advertising copy that reflected someone else's thoughts and ideas, and I did it to meet someone else's deadlines. With the creative awakening that ended that way of life, I found that the only way I was able to banish old associations that felt anything but free-flowing was to break all the patterns of my previous writing world.

First I abandoned the computer, composing *The MoonQuest*'s early drafts with pen and paper. Next, I abandoned my desk, bound as it was to the soul-numbing words that had so recently comprised my livelihood.

Most mornings immediately before or after breakfast, I allowed *The MoonQuest*'s scenes to pour from my pen onto the blank pages of the unlined pad balanced on my knee. Evenings, I input the day's jottings into my laptop, which migrated increasingly away from desks and toward sofas, beds, easy chairs and dining tables.

Some days I needed a more dramatic break from the old to connect with my nascent story. Already living in rural Nova Scotia by then, I would often drive over North Mountain to Baxters Harbour on the Bay of Fundy. There, as the Atlantic surf crashed on the rocky shore, I would sit in my car or on a boulder and let the ocean tell me what to write. That simple change of habit and venue was all it took to get me back on track.

When you feel blocked in your writing, one way to get unblocked is to break the pattern of your normal creative routine. Here are seven surefire suggestions:

1. Switch Writing Tools

Do you normally write on your computer? Get a writing app for your tablet or smartphone and go mobile. Where possible, use a cloud-linked version of the same app to ease your transition between devices.

Maybe it's time to set electronics aside altogether and pick up paper and pencil or pen. Not only did I write the first two drafts of *The MoonQuest* longhand, much of the initial draft of *The Voice of the Muse* was also a pen-and-paper undertaking. When we associate our computer (or tablet or phone) with work and the work isn't going well, the accompanying pressure can dam up our creative output. Relieve that pressure and reopen the floodgates.

If you already write longhand, switch from pen to pencil, or change pens or notepads. Or treat yourself to a special pen, special paper or a special notebook.

2. Speak It

Leave pen and computer behind and, instead, dictate your writing. These days, you don't need an assistant trailing behind you with a steno pad: Built into most of today's computers, tablets and smartphones are powerful speech-to-text capabilities. I often speak bits of whatever book I'm working on into my iPhone while I'm walking my dog, which combines this surefire suggestion with suggestions #4, #5 and #6. (Don't wait too long to go over the output, *without editing*, to correct the inevitable speech-to-text errors.)

3. Let Work Time Become Playtime

Change the font and text color in your writing application to something more inspiring and cheerful. Writing longhand? Use a colored pen or colored marker, as suggested in Section 2. Be playful, and turn your work time into playtime.

4. Try a New Time

When do you normally write? Change it. Write in the morning instead of the afternoon, or in the evening instead of the morning. Continue to experiment with writing times until you find a new one that feels right. Once you do, be open to changing it again. You may find, as I do, that different projects — even different drafts — make their own scheduling demands. With some of my books and screenplays, I have been more efficient and creative first thing in the morning. With others, mid-afternoon has worked best. My current project, a fifth story in my *Legend of Q'ntana* fantasy series, seems to want to alternate between mid-morning and late afternoon. The key is to listen, be flexible and trust that in this, too, your story knows best.

5. Ditch Your Desk

If you write at your desk, move away from the perceived pressures of your "work" environment. What's the most comfortable place in your home? Write there. I wrote large chunks of *The StarQuest* and *Acts of Surrender* on my living room couch or sitting up on my bed, and much of *The Bard of Bryn Doon* on my back patio. I have even been known to write in the bathtub.

6. Take a Break

Sometimes, the best way to shatter your existing routine is with a break. Go for a walk or a run to clear your mind. Take a shower or a leisurely bath. Take your dog to the park or, if you've got one nearby, the beach. Go to the gym. Do yoga, tai chi or other mindful exercise. Take a (non-writing) class. Visit a museum or art gallery. Take in a concert, movie or theater performance. Leave the planet altogether and find the nearest planetarium. Run errands. Go for a random drive or bus ride with no fixed destination. For me, a ten-minute walk around the block is sometimes all I need to get the words flowing again when I'm feeling stuck. Or take up other creative or artisanal pursuits — photography, sculpting or drawing, for example. Or quilting, woodworking or furniture restoration.

Do whatever you can do to keep your creative momentum alive until it's the right time to return to your writing.

¶ *See also "It Isn't Always Time to Write," later in this section.*

7. Leave Home

Get out of the house. Move your writing enterprise to a park, library or bookstore. Or head for your favorite café. Over the years, I've penned tens of thousands of words in coffeeshops. Alternatively, take yourself to somewhere scenic…quiet…different…inspirational, like I did at Baxters Harbour. Write outside if you can, or in the car if you prefer. Or take an aimless bus, train or subway ride and write along the way.

TRY THIS

Where do you normally write? At home? In a home office or study? Just for today, break that pattern. Take yourself and your writing somewhere you would never consider working. Sit in a park. Go to the zoo. Get on a boat. Drive to a scenic outlook and write in your car. Go to a beach, lakeshore or riverfront and write by the water. Pack a picnic and make a day of it. Take writing friends with you. Whatever it is, wherever you go and whomever you take along, let the experience be playful, fun and different.

AFTER YOU'VE WRITTEN

Did it work? Do it again next week, but go somewhere else and open yourself to another new experience of new rhythms and new routines.

Seven Surefire Tools for Transition

Sometimes, when we feel blocked, it's because we have not been able to move out of the logical, conventional, mind-centered universe in which we spend much of our time. Sometimes our day jobs keep us there. Sometimes our media or social media diets keep us there. Too often, our fear keeps us there.

When we're able to find ways to step away from that day-to-day outer world and into an inner space where listening, feeling and trusting are possible, we can more easily reconnect with our Muse and with our stories. That's important, because that place of connection is the place from which we create. The more disconnected we feel, the more we may need a transition ritual to ease us back into writing.

At its worst, as I noted in "Seven Surefire Ways to Rethink Your Writing Routine," ritual can become meaningless rote. At its best, however, it can act as a powerful vehicle of transition, carrying us from one state of mind and consciousness to another.

Pick one or several of the following transition rituals or devise your own. What is most important is that you remain open and adaptable to whatever will ease you into writing, recognizing that an individual practice may work for you once and never again.

Remember, the words always come. They come because they

are always present. Always. It is but for us to enter into that space of openness and receptivity where we can hear them.

1. A Special Place

Choosing a special place in which to write can be part of your ritual. That's particularly true in the early stages of a project or as you begin to unshackle yourself from the chains of silence and open more fully to the innate free-flow of your creativity.

A special place need not be a designated room, although if you can spare the space, a separate room can become a creative sanctuary that shifts your energy and lifts your mood the moment you step across its threshold.

If you cannot set aside an entire room, set aside a corner of a room or a favorite chair. Or make a space on your desk or next to your desk that is free from clutter, where you can set out whatever keepsakes help keep you connected to your writing. Perhaps it's an inspiring photo or art piece. Perhaps it's a favorite rock or crystal. Perhaps it's a favorite book. Set it out. Light a candle, incense or an aromatherapy burner, if that helps. The goal is to create an atmosphere uniquely yours that is conducive to creation.

If you are not able to use the same space each time you write, or choose not to do so, carry with you whichever keepsakes will inspire you wherever and whenever you feel called to write. I penned parts of *The Voice of the Muse* in my car, parked at a lookout about two-thirds of the way up Kohala Mountain on the Big Island of Hawaii. With me most days was a hand-painted keepsake box filled with meaningful treasures designed to rekindle my connection with my Muse. I stowed that same keepsake box in my cab when I was a taxi driver on Maui, working on *The StarQuest* between fares.

2. Music / Ambient Sound

Music can set a mood, support a feeling, enhance your creativity. It can also block out unwanted sounds from the street or from elsewhere in your home or apartment or condo building.

Everyone is different, and your music tastes may not be mine. When I work with music, I often prefer something meditative that is not too melodic, something that doesn't intrude too deeply into my consciousness. At the same time, different projects — even different drafts of the same project — have been known to make distinct musical demands.

For example, although the first edition of this book preferred baroque trumpet and choral music, much of this new edition was put together to the rhythms and grooves of smooth jazz. For my *Sara Stories* novels, which are set between the 1930s and 1990s, I wrote with the music of the period as a backdrop.

Discern what works for you and be flexible. What inspires you today may irritate you tomorrow. What animates you on one project or draft may stifle you on another.

3. Your Breath

After you sit down but before you begin to write, take a few minutes to breathe consciously and deeply, in and out. Breathe in the spirit and essence of your story. Breathe out all the stresses and distractions of your day. Breath into the writer you are. Breathe out everything unrelated to your writerly self. We have talked about breath before and will again. It's one of the best and easiest ways to come back to center and realign yourself with your story.

¶ *See also the Quick Centering Meditation under Transition Tool #6.*

4. Yoga / Exercise

Relaxing the body relaxes the mind and removes your focus from the day's pressures and demands. Yoga, tai chi and other Eastern-inspired practices work well. But five or ten minutes of simple stretching or other exercises can achieve the same end. If you don't already have an exercise practice, look online for free instructional videos.

However you choose to exercise, spend extra time on your neck, shoulders and eyes, all of which tighten easily when you're writing...or resisting. Shaking out your hands and wrists and your feet and ankles can also be helpful, as is anything that relieves tension from your lower back, where we all hold much of our resistance to change.

5. Nature Walk...or Around the Block

Sometimes, something as simple as a brief meditative walk is all the transition you need to shift from the non-writing part of your day into the Muse Stream. Walk in nature, if it's available, or stroll around your neighborhood. Wherever you walk, use that time — and your breath — to release any anxieties that might interfere with your creative flow.

6. Guided Meditation

Record one of the meditations in this book, create your own or listen to a track from *The Voice of the Muse Companion: Guided Meditations for Writers*. (See "Guided Meditations" in Section 1 for more about the recording.)

Even if you're waiting for your kids in the car, commuting on a bus, train or subway, or traveling in an airplane, you can pull out your favorite notebook, select a meditative track from your smartphone's music app, take a few closed-eye breaths and allow yourself to be drawn into the magical realm of your creativity.

Alternatively, practice using the following quick centering meditation until you can do it unprompted.

Quick Centering Meditation

Sit down — at your desk, in your favorite chair, in your favorite part of the garden, in your favorite park or on your favorite beach...wherever you feel comfortable, safe and inspired. Close your eyes, place your hands on your empty lap and breathe...in and out slowly, as slowly as you can, for ten breaths.

Breathe more slowly with each breath and feel your body relax. Feel each in-breath connect you to your story, your creative source or your Muse. Feel each out-breath flush all fear, doubt and anxiety from your system, flush all worldly concerns from your mind.

Focus on your heart and breathe into that space, into that fire, into that passion, into that well of creativity. Breathe into the writing you intend to begin or continue. Breathe into the light and life and heart of it. Breathe into your heart connection with it. Breathe into your vision for it. Breathe into your truth.

Breathe in, breathe out and listen. If you find yourself ready to dive onto the blank page or screen before your ten breaths are up, go for it. This is not about fixed rules. This is about getting you primed. Once you're primed, leap onto the page and let the words spill out of you.

This is also a great way to recenter when you find yourself stressed or distracted in the midst of your writing...or at any other time.

7. Reconnect with Your Vision

Whether we are conscious of it at the time, there is always an "inciting vision" that prompts us to start telling our story or a creative spark that ignites our passion to answer the call to write. Reconnecting with that creative spark or inciting vision is one of the best methods around for easing the transition from mind-centered to Muse-centered. And the best way to rekindle that connection is with the vision statement you crafted in Section 5. If you haven't yet created a vision statement, now's a great time to do it.

As I mentioned in Section 5, your vision statement can also help reignite a dimmed or extinguished creative spark. If you're feeling stuck and nothing else is working, spend time with your vision statement. As always, it's best to read your vision statement slowly and with feeling, aloud where possible and multiple times should you not feel its effect after the first time.

Finally...

Remember the "special gift" your Muse gave you at the end of the "Meet Your Muse" meditation (Section 3)? Incorporate that into any of the above transition rituals.

¶ *See also "Listen for the Voice of Your Muse," Section 9.*

4. Strive for Excellence, Not Perfection

In nature, perfection arrives in the instant preceding the start of decay. In nature, perfection breathes but a single breath, barely surviving the span of a lone heartbeat. In nature, perfection signals the beginning of the end...of everything.

There is no success beyond perfection. There is no future beyond perfection. There is no life beyond perfection.

There is nothing beyond perfection.

There is everything beyond excellence. Worlds of possibility. Galaxies of possibility. Infinite realms of possibility.

The pursuit of excellence frees you to keep growing. The pursuit of excellence frees you to keep learning. The pursuit of excellence frees you to keep creating. The pursuit of excellence frees you to keep succeeding.

Strive for excellence, not perfection.

Embrace Imperfection

Whether in writing or in life, many of us are addicted to getting it right. Being perfect, we believe, guarantees that we won't be criticized, won't be judged, won't be humiliated, won't be rejected. Being perfect means getting it right in a single draft. Being perfect means a six-figure publishing or production deal.

Okay, so that single-draft opus and six-figure deal may not happen (right away). Still, being perfect is, well, still a good thing to be. Isn't it?

Your writing may be excellent, accomplished, creative and insightful. It may be brilliant, compelling and universally lauded. But perfect? Not possible...no matter how hard you try and how many drafts you churn out. It isn't possible because no exact or perfect way exists to translate the intangible (ideas, thoughts, visions), the infinite (energy) and the dynamic (neural impulses) into the tangible, finite and static (language).

Can you describe the most stunning sunset you have ever experienced in words that accurately and precisely convey to me every shade and nuance of what you saw and felt? What about the birth of your first child or the death of a parent? Of course, you can't. Until we can beam what's in your brain and heart directly into mine, the "translation" can only ever be approximate, imprecise and imperfect — more an Impressionist painting than a hyperreal photograph.

That's okay. Those spaces between your Impressionist brushstrokes free me as reader to paint my own pictures from your descriptions, to have my own journey into your sunset, your birth or your death, to tap into my own feelings from your imperfectly expressed emotions.

Just as there is no way to control the words that flow from you onto the page and, at the same time, write from an authentic place of depth, there is no way you will ever be able to control your reader's experience of those words. Nor would you want to.

Empower your readers to have their own experiences. And recognize that all you can do is translate your experience as heartfully as you are able into the little squiggles on a page that we have agreed to act as imprecise outer symbols of our inner world. Begin by recognizing that most of the time you are only going to come close. Continue by knowing that it remains within your power to have your words incite revolution, topple dynasties, overthrow "reality."

Are you still intent on making your work perfect? Then you will likely find yourself stuck on the same story — or sentence or word — for the rest of your writing life, never growing into anything new...never growing into *any* definition of success.

Real success isn't built on perfection. Real success is built on qualities like excellence, persistence and risk-taking. It thrives on intuition and imagination. It embraces chaos and serendipity. It breaks the rules.

Real success is the antithesis of perfectionism, which demands order, insists on control, requires certainty.

In the end, the only certainty that perfectionism can produce is the certainty of frustration, if not despair. And the only certainty about success is that perfectionism is unlikely to get you there.

So don't beat yourself up — or your story — because it isn't perfect. Accept the inherent imperfection that is the perfection of all creative enterprise, and when you have done the best you can, let this story go and move on to your next.

Try This

Can you let go of your natural human perfectionism long enough to free your story to tell itself to you on the page? What are you waiting for? Pick up your pen. Describe what you see, what you feel, what you yearn for, what you love. Don't try to be perfect. Don't try at all. Simply allow. And know that from that place of surrender, you are creating the nearest thing possible to perfection.

Try This Too

Before you sit down to write, say aloud: "As the creator I am, I allow my words and work to emerge into their natural form and flow into *their* idea of perfection, not mine. I surrender to the story and let it flow." Now...let it flow.

Exploration

Ask yourself these questions (and answer honestly!)...

- Do I surrender to the Muse Stream as I write, or do I stop to go back over sentences and paragraphs trying to perfect them?

  If it's the former, keep up the good work and find a way to acknowledge the achievement; revisit Section 4's "Rule" #11 ("Set Yourself Up for Success") if you need a reminder about how important it is to celebrate your successes. If it's the latter, revisit "Floating Freely on the Muse Stream" in Section 2.

- Am I judging what I write as not good enough?

  If you are, notice your judgments, don't judge yourself for them and keep writing — through and past your judgment. Need help getting to a place of non-judgment? Revisit Section 4's "Let Judgment Go...and Let Your Story Flow" meditation ("Rule" #8).

The Pain of Perfection

In my *Acts of Surrender* memoir, I share the story of the powerfully evocative dream that did more than inspire me to start teaching. It compelled me to start. In short, my mentor had repeatedly asked me to teach a section of her ten-week writing course at the University of Toronto and I repeatedly said no...until I had the dream and had no choice but to say yes.

When it came time for me to prepare for the first class, I was determined to not only get it right, but to get it perfect. That way, I would be certain to not fail.

My Muse would have none of it: I had barely begun scripting out my presentation in comprehensive, exhaustive detail when my hands cramped up — so painfully that I couldn't type.

I laughed grimly at the irony of my predicament. The course was all about free-flow and spontaneity, about an organic, intuitive approach to creativity that was the antithesis of perfectionism's stifling choke hold. And here I was, so desperate to be word-perfect that I had been sucking the life from the class...and from me.

Reluctantly and with considerable terror, I knew that when I faced those strangers in that classroom, I would have to trust my mentor's training and my inner resources to guide me. That sounded good in theory. In practice? The mile walk to my first class felt like a death march.

A few minutes from the classroom, I paused on a terrace overlooking the campus. My heart thumped. My breath raced.

Eyes closed, I clutched the stone balustrade and attempted a fast-forward run-through of the class. My brain refused to cooperate, broadcasting instead a cacophony of crazed static.

"Breathe," I heard myself say softly through the din. "Slowly."

I slowed my breath as much as I could, which wasn't a lot, and found that if I stopped trying to anticipate the class, the static would stop. After a few minutes, I managed to release my grip and continue toward the classroom.

Somehow, I would make it through the evening. Somehow, I would get past my perfectionism. Somehow, I would do my best, and that would have to be good enough.

As it turned out, it was more than good enough: Those ten weeks raced by in a blur of creative flow — mine and my students'. By the final night, I was hooked. How could I have refused to teach? And once I had embraced the challenge, how could I have insisted that the experience be perfectly mapped and, well, stagnant?

By abandoning my fear-based perfectionism and allowing my best efforts to be good enough, I experienced some of the most profoundly transformative moments of my life to that point. If tension and a controlling need to be perfect had crippled my hands while preparing for my first class, by week ten I had relaxed into the same intuitive free-flow I was teaching.

Perfection is no more possible in your writing than it is in your life, so embrace the perfect imperfection of your creativity and your humanity.

Even Mary Poppins, that consummate nanny, claimed only to be "practically perfect." And as Salvador Dalí[1] once counseled, "Have no fear of perfection; you'll never reach it."

¶ *For more on kicking your perfectionism habit, see my book "The Way of the Imperfect Fool: How to Bust the Addiction to Perfection That's Stifling Your Success…in 12½ Super-Simple Steps."*

EXPLORATION

Ask yourself this question in your *Writer's Block Unblocked* journal, but don't think about the answer. Let it emerge freely and honestly on the Muse Stream:

- Where has my attachment to perfection blocked or sabotaged my creativity?

As Good as It Gets

Should you find any typos or grammatical errors in this "Strive for Excellence, Not Perfection" chapter or should you find any sentences or paragraphs here that don't flow as smoothly as they might, it's because by some Muse-inspired irony, I found myself spending more time

---

[1] The quote has also been attributed to scientist Marie Curie.

fussing with these few pages in my final read-through than with any other part of the book. So when it finally struck me that I was trying to perfect my words on perfection, I stopped fussing and moved on.

For this chapter, at least, this is as good as it gets!

5. Learn to Tell the Write Time

Recognize that what appears to be a block may be a matter of timing. If you have written as deeply into a story as you can and find yourself unable to continue, it may be that you need more life experience (or research) before you are ready to go on.

Instead of labeling yourself "blocked," welcome the break...to do research, to work on a different project or to get on with your life, trusting that you will know when the time is right to get back to it.

It Isn't Always Time to Write

A damp, wintry wind was gusting off the white-capped sapphire waters of Pubnico Harbour the afternoon I placed my stack of *MoonQuest* pages on a corner of my kitchen table. Through the three months of preparing to leave Toronto for rural Nova Scotia and my first two months in my new home, I hadn't looked at the manuscript. (See "Put Away Your Journal" in Section 6.)

Now I stared at it — through dinner that night, through breakfast the next morning and through lunch the following noon — not daring to touch it. Thing is, I was terrified to read those hundred pages. I was afraid the manuscript wasn't any good. I was also afraid that, through my months of transformative upheaval, I had outgrown the book and would have no choice but to abandon it.

With lunch that second day over, I gingerly picked up the printed pages and carried them to my favorite armchair. Optimist that I was, I also brought a pen and notepad with me.

What I realized, once I let myself begin reading, was that, even without Nova Scotia, I could never have continued with *The MoonQuest* all those months earlier. I hadn't been ready. The story had been more emotionally, spiritually and creatively mature than I was. That's why my Muse had write cut me off when it did.

As it turned out, those five world-altering months offered up precisely the life experience I needed in order to catch up with the story and carry on. I began writing the moment I finished reading, and three months and three hundred additional pages later, I dropped the final period on that first draft.

Sometimes, what seems like a block is a matter of timing. Sometimes, it's not the right idea. (See "Is Your Write Idea the Right Idea for You?" later in this section.) When we drop a project or leave it incomplete, we don't always know into which of those two categories it has fallen.

If your discernment tells you to let the project go, don't mourn the perceived waste of time and energy. Trust that you will either return to it when the time is right, or that you have gained all you required from the experience and can now move on to other writing.

No words you write are ever wasted. They are always stepping stones on the journey to better words, a better draft or a better project. They are always stepping stones on the journey to personal growth and transformation.

Exploration

Ask yourself these questions in your *Writer's Block Unblocked* journal, but don't think about the answers. Let them emerge freely and honestly on the Muse Stream. Let yourself be surprised by the answers.

- Am I forcing a project to completion when, perhaps, it's time to let it go for now...or for good?
- How can I be more discerning...about my work, about my passion, about my timing?

6. Rekindle Your Passion

If you're feeling stuck, ask yourself whether the story you're trying to write is one that excites and impassions you, one that fires you up more than anything else you could be writing. Is it the right idea for you right now? Or is it merely another good idea that anyone could write?

If you have lost the excitement (or never had it) and cannot rekindle (or find) your enthusiasm, consider that this may not be the best project for you at this time...or ever.

Lack of passion is a guaranteed recipe for stuckness. Passion, on the other hand, will always fuel your writing.

Is Your Write Idea the Right Idea for You?

There are many good ideas out there — ideas for books, short stories, stage plays and screenplays, ideas for songs, essays, articles and poems. Your friends will suggest them. Your spouse will suggest them. Your mother will suggest them. Your brother will suggest them. Your kids will suggest them. Everyone who knows you're a writer will suggest them.

More than anyone else, though, your logical mind will suggest them.

You see something online, on TV or in a magazine or newspaper, or you overhear something on the subway, in the supermarket or in a café, and you're convinced that whatever it is will make a bestselling novel or a blockbuster film, and that *you* are the writer to do it.

Maybe it would make a terrific story. Maybe it is yours to write.

Maybe it isn't.

There's a difference between a good idea and the right idea, between an idea that is anyone's for the taking and one that's uniquely yours, one that's right for you, right now.

Before you launch into a frenzy of research and writing, ask yourself: Is this what I feel driven to write? Is this the call of my Muse, the story only I can tell? Or is this anyone's story? Is this another good idea, or is this the *right write* idea for me?

Anyone can take a good idea and give it shape and substance. Some can do it better than you, some not as well.

No one can take the idea that sings to your soul and perform the kind of alchemy on it that you can. Only you can transform that idea into the one-of-a-kind gem it longs to be. That is why it, through your Muse, called to you...chose you.

Accept that you were chosen. Perform your magic. Let *your* right idea be the idea you write.

A wrong idea isn't necessarily wrong for all time. But if it's wrong for right now, let it go and free yourself to write what's right. For you. Right now.

Exploration

Ask yourself these questions in your *Writer's Block Unblocked* journal, but don't think about the answers. Let them emerge freely and honestly on the Muse Stream. Let yourself be surprised by the answers.

- How do I feel about the project that is going nowhere, the project that is making me feel blocked? Does it fire me up? Is it something I care passionately about? Or is it merely another idea?

- If it fires me up, what's holding me back? How can I use the tools in this book to reinspire myself? What else can I do to rekindle my passion?

- If it's a write idea but not the *right* idea, why have I devoted so much energy to it? Can I let it go and move on?

7. Say "Yes" to You

Remember "Rule" #8 from Section 4? Love yourself and your words... every draft. That's right, *every* draft. Treat each draft as you would your child — with love and without judgment, recognizing that gentle correction might be required along its journey to maturity...recognizing, too, that any correction must always come from a foundation of compassion and respect.

The more you beat yourself up over your writing output or creative ability, the more you invite the kind of paralysis that feeds writer's block.

Discard judgment and punishing discipline. Cultivate discernment and discipleship. Recognize that every word, draft and emotion is an integral part of your creative journey...of your life's journey. Honor all aspects of that journey, including the painfully uncomfortable ones, and writer's block will become little more than a myth.

Know Thyself

Are you discovering things about yourself or your beliefs through your writing that make you uncomfortable? Are you reluctant to let your story carry you into new, potentially dangerous territory?

Creative expression is about self-discovery. We don't write what we know so much as we write to discover what we know, to discover what we believe, to uncover hidden depths within ourselves that only emerge when we take a leap of faith onto the blank page and write freely from our heart. Writing on the Muse Stream is one tool for accomplishing that.

"Most writers write to say something about other people — and it doesn't last," Gloria Steinem wrote in *Revolution From Within*. "Good writers write to find out about themselves, and it lasts forever."

Where are you hiding behind your words? From yourself and from others.

Where are you letting yourself shine through your words? For yourself and for others.

There's a difference between self-indulgently puking your life onto the page and self-revealingly using your life and emotions to connect with your readers. Don't censor yourself, but learn to discern when your experiences have universal value and when they serve only you. Both deserve to be written. Only the former deserves to be shared.

Exploration

Ask yourself these questions in your *Writer's Block Unblocked* journal, but don't think about the answers. Let your answers emerge freely and honestly, writing them on the Muse Stream in a free-flowing, stream-of-consciousness way where appropriate. Let yourself be surprised by the answers.

- Where am I hiding behind my words? Where am I hiding from myself? Where am I hiding from others?
- Where am I letting myself shine through my words? For myself and for others?

Dare to Create. Dare to Write.

Creative artists are innovators. Creative artists are trailblazers. Creative artists journey off the edge of the earth, to those places where maps of old warned, "Here, there be dragons."

Your job as a creative artist is to write what yearns to be released from you onto the page. Not as others have done it in the past. Not as others tell you to do it. But as only you can: with your unique history, outlook, style and voice.

Don't write what you think you should. Write what you must. Write it as only it can be written. Write it as only you can write it. Write it now.

Say "Yes" to Your Muse
A Quick Meditation

If you have not yet created a vision statement (Section 5), or even if you have, let this quick exercise keep you aligned with your writer self and connected with your writing projects.

Allow 5 minutes for this meditation.

Close your eyes. Take a few deep breaths, in and out, in and out, breathing out whatever distractions surround you, whatever you were doing, thinking or saying before this moment.

Now, breathe in the essence of your creative self, the fire that is your creative self.

Breathe in your book, your screenplay, your stage play, your short story, your essay, your song or your poem — whatever your current project is, if you have one. If you don't have a current project, breath in to your creative essence, to the writer you are.

Breathe in your Muse. Breathe in the knowledge that you are a writer of power, strength and substance. See a flame or white light in your heart center, that energy center in the middle of your chest. See it and breathe into it.

Connect with your Muse and assure it that you *will* sit down to write. Commit to a time. Commit to a place. Keep your appointment. Keep your commitment.

Try This

You know what to do. Don't wait for the perfect moment that will never come. Don't wait until you have one, two or five free hours. Don't wait for the perfect idea or the perfect opening sentence. Don't wait until you have an outline. Don't wait until you take a writing class. Don't wait until you finish reading this chapter. Now is the best time to write. Return to an existing project or pick a keyword or key phrase at random or from "Seventy Keys to Unlock Your Muse Stream" (Section 3), set your timer for 10 or 20 minutes and get writing. Say *yes* to your Muse!

9. The Soul of Creation

To see a candle's light, one must take it into a dark place.
URSULA K. LE GUIN

Every author in some way portrays himself in his works, even if it be against his will.
GOETHE

Pre-Conception

Your story exists. I know it's hard to believe when all you see in front of you is a blank page or an empty screen. I know it's hard to believe when you gaze down at your virginal white sheet or stare at the pixel blinking at you accusingly and nothing is there — no words, no ideas... nothing. I know it's hard to believe when no hint presents itself of which key to press to get started, or which letter to form to launch your story's journey from conception to creation.

The emptiness terrifies you. Of course, it does. "You're not a writer," it shrieks. "If you were, you would know how to start."

Your doubts deepen. "How can there be a story inside me? Why can't I see it? Why can't I know it? Is it even real?"

Your story is real. It's as real as you are. Believe in it as it believes in you. Be ready for it, for it has long been ready for you.

How?

Learn to listen for your story. Learn to listen *to* your story. It will materialize...as first one word, then another; as first one sentence, then another; as first one page, then another. Then another.

It will materialize if you let it, if you let its words spill out of you, if you let its words continue to spill out of you until the story is written.

It will materialize if you let it. Let it.

Listen for the Voice of Your Muse

As I have mentioned previously, your Muse is always present and always available, whether you are sitting absolutely still or rocking to your favorite band. At the same time, it can take practice to hear the voice of your creative source clearly through the busy babel of everyday life. What follows are seven surefire ways to help you be more receptive.

It's no accident some of these overlap with "Seven Surefire Tools for Transition" under Surefire Solution #3 (Section 8). Transition time is also about preparing to listen.

1. **Meditate**: Do you have a daily meditation practice? Those twenty minutes can help you open to that still, small voice that isn't so small. Remember, though, that it's not how often you meditate, it's whether you can train yourself to live your life as a meditation. Alternatively, use any of this book's meditation scripts, recording it for yourself or having someone read it to you.
2. **Get out into Nature**: Find a park, nature trail or other quiet spot where you can sit in the stillness or go for an impromptu amble.
3. **Get Moving**: Go for a run or a workout.
4. **Get Wet**: Soak in the tub or take a long shower.
5. **Go for a Walk or Drive**: Anywhere. The more random, the better. It will help clear your head.
6. **Exercise Yourself**: Take up yoga, tai chi or some other centering discipline that is at once physical and meditative.
7. **Exercise Your Passion**: When we immerse ourselves in our passion, we often enter into a Zen moment of presence and receptivity. What passions do you have apart from writing? It could be a traditionally creative passion, or it could as easily be found in your kitchen, workshop, garden or kids' playroom.

The Soul of Creation

A Guided Meditation

Allow at least 20 minutes to complete this meditation and for the writing that flows from it.

My studio recording of this meditation is available for download or streaming as part "The Voice of the Muse Companion: Guided Meditations for Writers." See "Guided Meditations" in Section 1 ("Getting Started") to find out how to access the recording, as well as for tips on how best to use this book's meditations.

Relax. Close your eyes. Return to that meditative space where all is possible, where judgments are dissolved, where creativity is sovereign.

Feel again that place in your heart where the creator within you resides, that place through which your Muse speaks. That place of light and of life. That eternal place. That magical place.

That place where everything is possible. Where creation is possible. Where magic and mystery and spirit and flow are the natural and normal ways of being.

Breathe into that, into that space.

Breathe into the power of your voice, your heart, and the expression, through your voice, of your heart.

And voice becomes words. And words become scratches on a page that, with the miracle of creation, become a whole — sometimes in spite of you. So, surrender to that place of miracle and magic. That place of creation.

Breathe into it deeply and become one with it. So that when you reach for your pen and touch it to the page, or set your fingers on the keyboard, the words flow effortlessly.

And remember how important it is, always, to go with whatever comes first into your mind, whatever flows from your heart to your hand.

Now, reach deep inside, past the censoring of your mind, past the fear of your personality self, and let a word or an image emerge that represents creation for you.

The soul of creation.

Whatever that word or image is will be unique to you and to this moment. And it will be perfect.

Remember that what you write may be about this or about something else altogether. This word is a jumping-off point, a place of departure on a magical, miracle-filled journey that you will discover in the writing.

Surrender to the journey. Surrender to the word or image that launches it. Surrender to the story.

Allow yourself to be carried effortlessly and weightlessly, lovingly and supportively, in the embrace of your creativity, as you write this word on the page and allow it to take you into the realm of your divinity, the kingdom of your creation.

When you're ready, but only then, open your eyes, remaining in that place you now find yourself, and write the word or image that came to you, that rose from deep within you.

Set it to paper and allow it to become the launching pad for that rocket-propelled journey that takes you where you need to go, where deep in your heart you desire to go...into the soul of creation.

So, when you're ready, take off and go. Take off and write.

Remember to keep going, nonstop, until you sense completion — writing through and past all stuckness, allowing creation to birth through you and onto the page.

A Story is Born

It's March 1994. I see *The Celtic Tarot* card deck in Toronto's Omega Centre bookstore, and it so seduces me that I can't walk away from it, even though I don't know how to read tarot and have no conscious desire to learn. What I am learning, though, is to trust my intuition, so after several attempts to leave the store empty-handed, I reluctantly surrender, despite the deck's discomfiting price tag.

A few mornings later, I'm preparing for a writing workshop I am to teach when *The Celtic Tarot* catches my eye from across the room. As I thumb through the deck with its evocative cards, I realize why I had to have it: I will use it as part of a writing exercise for the workshop.

That evening, I have each student draw, closed-eyed, one of the major arcana cards. I then have them open their eyes as I guide them through a meditative journey into writing.

Everyone launches into a frenzy of creative output and I'm relieved, not only because the exercise is working but because it has justified my extravagant purchase.

I rarely write during a workshop that I'm facilitating. Instead, I keep an eye on participants in case anyone needs help. This class is different. Within moments, some inner imperative insists that I also draw a card. I reach into the deck and pull out the Chariot.

Without full awareness of what I'm doing, I pick up my pen, pull my notepad toward me and start to write. What emerges, after a rambling preamble, is the tale of an odd-looking man in an odd-looking coach. Pulling the coach are horses as oddly colored as those on the Chariot card.

I know nothing about this man and his horses. I know nothing about this story. All I know is what emerges, word by word, onto the page.

Next morning, lured back into the story, I add to it. I continue adding to it daily, almost obsessively, rarely knowing from one day to the next where this unusual tale is carrying me. A year later on the anniversary of that Toronto class and a thousand miles away in a tiny Nova Scotia village, I complete the first draft of a fantasy novel I never expected to write: *The MoonQuest*.

Postscript

It's May 2007, twenty-eight hundred miles away and many drafts and years later. I open my email to an attachment from Courtney Davis, the British artist who created *The Celtic Tarot*[1]. The image is the Chariot card, which I haven't seen since I gifted my copy of the deck to a tarot-reader friend in 1997. Davis has sent me a JPEG to tweak my memory so I can write a caption for it, for an upcoming retrospective of his art.

When I see the Chariot for the first time in a decade, I'm startled. Even though the artist who designed *The MoonQuest*'s first-edition cover never saw the tarot card and knows nothing of *The Celtic Tarot* or how it inspired me, I notice a marked similarity between the two. Not only are the horses identically colored, they are identically placed. There is even a tiny chalice tucked above the wording on the card.

Although I have retired that original cover, the Chariot's inspiration remains evident throughout *The MoonQuest* — a story that knew itself far better than I did...a story that knew me better than I knew myself...a story that insisted I trust it to reveal itself to me, moment by moment, word by word...a story that has never let me down.

Exploration

Ask yourself these questions in your *Writer's Block Unblocked* journal, but don't think about the answers. Let them emerge freely and honestly...on the Muse Stream, where appropriate. Let yourself be surprised by the answers.

- How can I trust my story to reveal itself to me?
- How can I surrender more fully to the mystery of the blank page?
- Can I write the story that wants to be written by me, even if I don't yet know what it is?
- Can I start? Now? *Need help? Turn to the next chapter.*

---

[1] Sadly, the Courtney Davis *Celtic Tarot* that birthed *The MoonQuest* is now out-of-print, although you can still find used and collectable editions online.

Birthing Your Story
A Guided Journey

This is a version of the meditative exercise that birthed "The MoonQuest." For it, you will need a selection of evocative images, preferably ones toward which you have no conscious emotional connection. For example:

- *Any divination or oracle deck. If it's a tarot deck where the minor arcana comprise only numbers, as was the case with "The Celtic Tarot," separate out the major arcana cards and use only those.*
  - *Images clipped from a magazine or printed from the internet.*
    - *A coffee table book of photography or art reproductions.*
    - *A writing colleague's family photo album or travel pics.*
      - *A stranger's Instagram or other photo feed.*

Alternatively, go to a museum, an art gallery or a sculpture garden and park yourself on a bench with a good view of several works of art. Then adapt the following exercise to your location.

♪ ♪ ♪

This exercise is designed to get you writing, so have pen and paper, tablet or computer within easy reach.

Allow at least 40 minutes for this meditation and for the writing experience that flows from it.

Find a quiet place where you won't be disturbed, and get comfortable. Close your eyes, take a few deep breaths, in and out, and relax.

Breathe in to your creative source, whatever that is for you, and breathe out all doubt, fear and judgment.

Place your palm against your heart and breathe in to your heart, then breathe out everything that is not heart. Let your breath wash away all anxiety, stress or strain. Let it wash away all feelings that you must control this experience.

Breathe in deeply, and let yourself surrender fully to this moment... and now to this one.

Continue to focus on your breath and, remaining in a meditative space, open your eyes.

If you are working with loose images (cards, photos, etc.), shuffle them at least three times, keeping them face down. When you feel ready, pick a card or photo, but don't look at it yet.

If you are working with a book or album, open it at random, bookmarking the selected page with your finger. But don't open the book to look at the image.

If you are working with an Instagram or other photo feed, keep your eyes closed as you use your finger or mouse to blindly scroll up and down the screen to select an image. Turn away from the device so as not to see what you chose.

If several original art pieces are arrayed before you, pick either the one you are the least familiar with, the one that tugs at you or the third from the right. As with a random keyword or key phrase, the work you pick is less important than the act of creative surrender that follows.

Close your eyes again for a few moments and return your focus to your breath. Breathe in and out a few more times, as deeply as you can.

Now, focus your breath on the image or art piece you have selected, even if you have not yet seen it. Breathe in to it. Feel yourself connect with it. Become one with it, whatever it is.

Remaining in that meditative space, gently open your eyes. Continue to focus on your breath as you breathe into your image and either turn over your chosen card or picture, open your book or album to the page you have bookmarked, or focus on your chosen art piece.

Before looking at your image or art piece closely, I would like you to simply take it in. The whole thing. An overview. As though you are gazing down on a landscape that is miles below you, as though you are looking down from an alpine summit or from an airplane window. Ignore the details for now. Take it in. Breathe it in.

Ask yourself these questions, now and throughout your experience with this image or art piece, and censor nothing. Let yourself be surprised by the answers.

- How does the image or art piece make me feel?
- What emotions does it evoke?
- What physical sensations does it arouse?
- Does it trigger any thoughts or memories? Any associations? Anything else?
- Does it make me uncomfortable in any way? How?
- Alternatively, is it comforting or reassuring in some way? How?

Now, still ignoring its specifics, take in the colors, hues, shadows and shadings of the piece. Its shapes. Its areas of brightness. Its areas of dark. And everything in between.

Remember to keep breathing, deeply.

What do you feel now? And now?

Now it's time to zoom in to the specifics of the image or art piece, to its details.

What is your first thought as you look at it more closely?

Look at it more closely still. Notice details you might have missed previously. Let your eyes slowly spiral into the center of the image or art piece, starting in the lower left corner and continuing counterclockwise until you get to the center.

Rest for a few breaths at its center, then return in a clockwise direction back to the outer edges.

As you travel the image or art piece in this way, be aware of what you notice and feel.

When you have completed your two circuits, back up to a middle view.

Whether the image or art piece is realistic or abstract, imagine it in motion. What does that look like? What story does it tell?

Now, step inside the image or art piece. Step inside it and engage with it in whatever way feels right. As you do, bring all your senses into play.

Don't judge or second-guess. Experience what you experience, and surrender into it.

- What do things look like from the inside? In what ways are they different than they were from the outside?
- What do you see beyond the frame of your image or beyond the physicality of your art piece that is invisible from the outside?

- What smells do you smell?
- What can you reach out and touch? What does it feel like?
- What can you taste or imagine tasting?
- What do you hear?
- Is there anyone (or anything) you can interact with? If so, do it.

Surrender fully into this part of the exercise and give yourself all the time you need for it. When you are complete, continue on to the final portion.

Now, step back outside the image or art piece, return to where you were at the start of the exercise and take one last look into your image or art piece. Notice anything you might have missed previously. Note any emotions or associations you didn't feel earlier. Be aware of any new physical sensations.

If you already know what you feel called to write from the experience, go ahead and start. If you are unsure, let one of your impressions or experiences of the image or art piece be the key that unlocks your creative journey. Alternatively, use the key phrase, "This image/painting/sculpture is…" or "This image/painting/sculpture says…" or "This image/painting/sculpture could be…"

Remember to write on the Muse Stream, without stopping. If you get stuck, keep your pen moving — through repetition, free association or nonsense words or by describing the image or art piece. Remember, too, to be aware of your breath.

As you write, ignore all concerns about spelling, punctuation or grammar. Don't worry if what you are writing seems to make no sense or seems to have nothing to do with anything you thought you might want to write about. Start, and let the writing carry you where it will — into a new story, deeper into an existing story or on a journey whose aim and destination will make themselves known to you in their way and in their time.

10. Other Perspectives

You must be prepared to work always without applause.
Ernest Hemingway

The important thing is never to let oneself be guided
by the opinion of one's contemporaries; to continue steadfastly
on one's way without letting oneself be either
defeated by failure or diverted by applause.
Gustav Mahler

Sympathetic Vibrations

Feedback (noun): sympathetic vibration...
Roget's International Thesaurus

There is a time to hold your words and work to yourself and a time to begin sharing them out into the world. Only you can know which time is which. Only you can discern how, when and with whom to begin the process.

Feedback is part of that sharing process. It involves *selectively* sharing your work in order to receive what will help you strengthen your writing and support you in your creativity. Selectively, because not everyone will be able to supply you with what you require, and not everyone will support you in the ways you need and desire.

Notice that I avoid words like "criticism" and "critique." For many, these words carry an emotional charge of harshness and negativity, even of cruelty. Words, as Alice discovered in Wonderland, bear the meanings we believe them to carry far more than they do their strict dictionary definitions. To me, "feedback" carries with it the potential of a positive, supportive response, of a sympathetic vibration.

Ultimately, however, the tone and tenor of any solicited response to your work is up to you. Are you seeking sympathetic vibrations or are you opening yourself to that other, less supportive definition of feedback, "unwanted noise"? It's that second type of feedback that can too easily trigger creative blocks and shutdowns.

This is your work, your creative process. You have the right and the obligation to choose when you will seek feedback and from whom. You also have the right and the obligation to select the precise nature and level of feedback you will receive.

You cannot control your creative journey, but you can empower yourself in it.

The Seven Be's of Empowered Feedback

Empower yourself in your creative process by following these guiding principles when sharing your work with anyone.

1. Be Selective

Your work is as much your creation as is your child. You have no more right to knowingly expose it to influences that could harm it or set it back than you do your child. This is especially true if you have felt blocked in the past. Seek out only those people who will support you and your writing. Never assume that those closest to you will fall into that category. Often, without intending to hurt you, they are the most critical and least helpful.

When someone asks to read your writing, always use your discernment when considering the request, and give yourself permission to say no when appropriate.

This applies equally to writers' groups. Get a sense of the group before joining and, once you are attending, note the type of feedback offered by its members before agreeing to share your work. The only reason to offer feedback is to support the writer and his or her work. Not all groups and individuals subscribe to that philosophy.

¶ *See "Creative Connection" later in this section for detailed suggestions on how to set up a writers' group.*

2. Be Open

Your work, like your child, requires fresh air and outside influences. Don't be overprotective and suffocating. Don't let fear hold you back from sharing your work and your vision. Be open to others' perceptions, comments and responses. At the same time, exercise discernment in determining which of those perceptions and comments are relevant and which can be dismissed at this moment in your work's development and yours.

3. Be Aware

To everything there is a season. At different stages in your work and in your creative process, you will be ready to hear different things. Respect where you are and seek only the type and depth of feedback you are prepared to receive, integrate and apply. Recognize when you are at your most raw and respect that too. As always, discernment is key.

4. Be Clear

Be clear within yourself about the type of feedback that you require and desire at this stage on your journey with your writing. For example:

- Do you want to know what emotions your work evokes? Does it trigger laughter? Tears? Terror? Is it gripping? Compelling?

- Do you want to know whether the reader is able to identify with your protagonist? Whether your characters are original and credible? Whether your dialogue is natural or appropriate? Whether your descriptions, imagery and settings are vivid and original? Whether your arguments are persuasive or convincing? Whether your sex scenes or scenes of violence are too graphic? Not graphic enough?

- Are you seeking detailed line-by-line input? Or are you interested in nothing but general comments?

- Are you seeking nothing more than a pat on the back for having completed a first draft...or for simply having written? That is also valid feedback.

Only you can determine what will support your creative process at this time and what might damage it, so...

5. Be Explicit

Once you have determined the type and depth of feedback that is appropriate for you at this time, ask for it — clearly, directly and with neither apology nor equivocation. Your reader cannot know how best to support you unless you make your needs clear.

Don't be shy or embarrassed to make those needs known. If you are vague or hesitant, you open yourself to comments you may not be ready to hear, comments that could feel hurtful or damaging, even if they are not intended to be so.

6. BE STRONG

Know what you want and don't be afraid to speak up — lovingly, compassionately and, again, without apology — when you are not getting it, or when you are getting something you didn't ask for. This is *your* creative process. You have every right to seek out what will help and support you as you bring your work to completion. In this, you are not only training yourself to seek out what will assist you, you are training your friends, family and fellow writers to provide feedback in supportive ways and to seek it for themselves in empowered ways.

7. BE DISCERNING

The words on your page are an expression of you, but they are not you. Negative comments, whether intentionally cruel or not, have no power to harm you unless you abdicate your power and allow yourself to be hurt...or blocked. Deep inside, you know your work's strengths and weaknesses. Tap into that intuitive inner knowingness and rely on it to discern which comments it is wisest to ignore and which support you and serve your story.

ASK YOURSELF THESE QUESTIONS WHEN SEEKING FEEDBACK

- How can I be clearer within myself about the feedback I need and with others about the feedback I am seeking?
- How can I be more discerning in to whom I turn for feedback?
- How can I be more respectful of my needs and my work's when seeking feedback?
- How can I be more discriminating in determining which feedback to take to heart and which to dismiss?

These Questions Too

- How easy is it for me to respond honestly to others' suggestions and expectations?
- Do I have people-pleasing tendencies that have found their way into what and how I write? Into how I relate to others about my work?
- How easy is it for me to trust my discernment?

The Seven Be's of Compassionate Feedback

Share these seven principles with those to whom you intend to show your work, and be certain that they are comfortable abiding by them. Read and commit to them yourself before commenting on a friend or colleague's work.

1. Be Constructive

Remember, the *only* reason to offer feedback is to support the writer and his or her work. This is not a test of your ability to pick out flaws. Don't be smart. Be gentle. Don't show off. Be fair.

2. Be Balanced

Always begin with the positive — with what you like about the piece, with its strengths, with what works for you. With that foundation of support, you can then offer constructive comments. Remember, you can say anything you feel called to say about the work as long as you frame it with respect and compassion and as long as you honor the parameters the writer set out when asking for feedback.

3. Be Mindful

Give only the type and level of feedback the writer has sought. If there are other elements you would like to comment on, ask permission. Respect the answer you get.

4. Be Respectful

You don't have to agree with the writer's premise and opinions to give constructive feedback. Nor is it your place to comment on them unless asked. If you don't feel you can respect the writer's approach and views, suggest, respectfully, that the writer seek feedback elsewhere.

5. Be Specific

You are at your most helpful when you can offer examples from the text of what works and what doesn't. Be clear.

6. Be Nurturing

Sometimes all a writer needs is praise for having written. Avoid the kind of question Nora Barnacle is said to have asked husband and *Ulysses* author, James Joyce: "Why don't you write books people can read?"

7. Be Compassionate

Remember the Golden Rule of Feedback and abide by it: "Speak unto others in the manner you would have them speak unto you." Put yourself in the writer's shoes and offer feedback as you would *honestly* prefer to receive it.

Ask Yourself These Questions When Offering Feedback

- How can I listen more clearly to the nature of the feedback that has been requested of me?
- How can I be clearer and more specific in the feedback I offer?
- How can I be more respectful of the work and its creator, offering feedback that doesn't show how smart I am but, instead, serves the needs and growth of the writer and his or her work?

Creative Connection

Too often, we don't recognize our creativity, can't see our talent, refuse to acknowledge our power. That's not surprising, given how solitary and insular writing can be, given how untrained so many people are in the words and actions that support creativity.

Groups can be a powerful antidote to that. Coming together with other writers offers you an opportunity to take all you have experienced and read in these pages and multiply it manyfold through the loving support of others.

One way to forge creative connection and build creative support is by starting a Voice of the Muse Writers' Circle, a concept I initiated with *The Voice of the Muse: Answering the Call to Write*. It's easy: Share your enthusiasm, your commitment and *Writer's Block Unblocked* with like-spirited writing colleagues and, voilà, you are part of a powerful vortex of motivation and inspiration.

These days, you and your fellow Circle members needn't be in the same city or the same part of the world. Social media sites make it easy to find writers who share your passion and outlook. And Zoom, FaceTime and other videoconferencing platforms make time-zone conflicts the sole barrier to creative connection across the miles.

However you format your Voice of the Muse Writers' Circle, consider including these seven elements, all geared toward keeping participants unblocked and in the flow:

1. Check-in

When dealing with creative blocks, mutual accountability can be a powerful motivator. Set aside time at every get-together for each member to share creative experiences since the last meeting. Here are some of the questions worth addressing:

- Are you writing?

- How/where are you finding time to write?
- Is writing getting easier?
- Which distractions, blocks or fears have you identified and overcome?
- What have you written this week?
- What were your successes?
- How did you transform your challenges into opportunities?

Keep contributions brief. This is not a time for mutual therapy, nor is it a time to make others feel guilty if they haven't written. It's a time for mutual support. You want to make sure that there is time for...

2. Writing

Set aside most of your time for writing and sharing. Pick or adapt an exercise from this or another of my writing books, create one yourself or use a track from *The Voice of the Muse Companion* recording. Then set a timer for twenty or thirty minutes and write.

3. Sharing

Allow whoever wants to share what they have written that opportunity. Share not only writing content but writing process. Make sure everyone is familiar with the points in the two "Seven Be's" chapters that precede this one. In the beginning, as you're getting to know each other and each other's work, focus more on general support than on detailed feedback.

4. Rotation

Avoid leader burnout by taking turns communicating with members, moderating the circle, hosting the circle and choosing the exercises.

5. Frequency

Agree to meet regularly. Weekly or every two weeks is ideal, but at least monthly.

6. Numbers

Keep the size of your group small enough so that everyone who wants to has an opportunity to share — if not at every meeting, then at every second or third meeting.

7. Other Ideas

- *Meeting in someone's home?* Create a space and ambiance conducive to creativity, one that's quiet and where you and your fellow members won't be disturbed. Make sure, for example, that all cellphones are switched off. If any participants are writing on laptops or tablets, ask them to mute or switch off all notification sounds. Consider playing meditative music as people arrive to set the atmosphere. Consider, too, using meditative music during writing time, but poll your members first, as some might prefer silence. People bond well over food, and many groups incorporate regular or occasional potlucks into their get-togethers.

- *Meeting online?* Make sure all members join your virtual circle from somewhere quiet where they won't be interrupted or disturbed. Encourage them to stay focused on the get-together by quitting all unnecessary applications and by muting all sounds unrelated to the group experience.

Remember, your Voice of the Muse Writers' Circle is designed to get you writing, keep you writing and support you in your creativity. Remember, too, that creativity at its best is a joyful experience. Write... and have fun!

11. On Rejection

Art is a wound turned into light.
Georges Braque

Better to write for yourself and have no public,
than to write for the public and have no self.
Cyril Connolly

Feeling Rejected? Don't Be Dejected

> *I received your rejection by email recently, which was surprising since I did not submit an application to the Art San Diego Short Film Program. Like most artists, I am accustomed to having my work rejected, but being rejected from something I did not enter is a new low.*
>
> SHAWNEE BARTON, SCREENWRITER

Unlike Shawnee Barton's, most rebuffs are not unsolicited. At the same time, few are the creative artists who never experience rejection. Author Madeleine L'Engle, for example, received twenty-six refusals, including one from her existing publisher, for her landmark young adult fantasy, *A Wrinkle in Time.*

Toward the end of that two-year period of steady rejections, L'Engle covered up her typewriter and decided to give up — on *A Wrinkle in Time* and on writing.

Technically, Madeleine L'Engle wasn't blocked. She was discouraged. But discouragement and feelings of failure can easily lead to an inability to write.

For L'Engle, that decision to throw in the towel was short-lived. Or, perhaps, a determined Muse caught L'Engle's towel and tossed it back at her: On her way downstairs to the kitchen, L'Engle had an epiphany — an idea for a novel about failure. In a flash, she was back at her typewriter.

"That night," as she explained thirty years later in a PBS documentary, "I wrote in my journal, 'I'm a writer. That's who I am. That's what I am. That's what I have to do — even if I'm never, ever published again.' And I had to take seriously the fact that I might never, ever be published again. ... It's easy to say I'm a writer now, but I said it when it was hard to say. And I meant it."

Once it was finally published in 1962, *A Wrinkle in Time* went on to win major awards and be translated into more than a dozen languages. It's now considered a classic and remains as popular as ever. Today, the bibliography on L'Engle's website lists some fifty works, including several published posthumously.

"I cannot possibly tell you how I came to write *A Wrinkle in Time*," her 2007 *New York Times* obituary quotes her as having said. "It was simply a book I had to write. I had no choice."

Try This

Has discouragement or fear of failure slowed or halted your creative output? If you are reading these words today, it's because writing and creative expression are important to you. Sure, you want to be published or produced. Who doesn't? But what's more important: a lucrative contract or the opportunity to release onto the page the stirrings of your soul? Yes, both would be terrific. Yet the former cannot happen *unless you are writing*.

So let's explore *why* you write.

Set aside 30 minutes for this exercise, in two 15-minute segments.

Kick off the first part of your writing with this phrase: "I am a writer because..." Allow yourself to explore all the reasons you feel called to write. Don't do it with your mind. Do it on the Muse Stream, from your heart.

For the second part of the exercise, begin with this phrase if you have a particular project you are feeling challenged by: "I am passionate about [*name of project*] because..." Otherwise, use this phrase: "I love to write about..."

Once again, remember to write on the Muse Stream. Remember, too, to write without stopping and without thinking. Let the words that find their way through you onto the page reveal truths you didn't know you knew. Let your writing be a journey of discovery as well as rediscovery.

Still Dejected? Here Are More of the Infamously Rejected

On New Year's Day 1962, the same day *A Wrinkle in Time* was finally published, Decca executives in London auditioned a little-known rock 'n' roll band for a grueling two hours and fifteen songs. After a two-week, nail-biting wait, the band's manager finally heard back from Decca's Dick Rowe: "Not to mince words, Mr. Epstein," Rowe wrote, "but we don't like your boys' sound. Groups are out; four-piece groups with guitars particularly are finished." The manager was Brian Epstein. The group, of course, was The Beatles.

Dick Rowe wasn't the only creative decision-maker forced to eat his words...

- Theodore Geisel's first book as Dr. Seuss was turned down twenty-seven times before landing a publishing contract. Geisel ultimately won a Pulitzer Prize and a Peabody Award, as well as two Oscars and a pair of Emmys.

- Jack Canfield and Mark Victor Hansen had Dr. Seuss beat: Their original *Chicken Soup for the Soul* book was rejected by more than a hundred publishers ("nobody wants to read a book of short little stories") before it launched a multimillion-dollar franchise.

- Publishing giant Alfred A. Knopf rejected Jack Kerouac's *On the Road*, dismissing it as a huge, sprawling and inconclusive novel that would attract small sales and garner indignant reviews.

- Knopf also rejected George Orwell's *Animal Farm* ("it is impossible to sell animal stories in the U.S.A."), as well as Sylvia Plath ("there certainly isn't enough genuine talent for us to take notice"), Anne Frank, Vladimir Nabokov and Isaac Bashevis Singer ("it's Poland and the rich Jews again"). Singer went on to win a Nobel Prize.

- Kurt Vonnegut, William Faulkner, Judy Blume, Jorge Luis Borges ("utterly untranslatable"), Norman Mailer ("this will set publishing back twenty-five years"), James Joyce and D.H. Lawrence also received multiple rejections before finally getting a yes.

- Other literary rebuffs? William Golding's *Lord of the Flies*, Oscar Wilde's *Lady Windemere's Fan*, Joseph Heller's *Catch-22*, Anita Loos's *Gentlemen Prefer Blondes*, John le Carré's *The Spy Who Came in from the Cold* ("you're welcome to le Carré — he hasn't got any future"), Stephen King's *Carrie* (rejected thirty times), Kenneth Grahame's *The Wind in the Willows* ("an irresponsible holiday story"), the original "Tarzan of the Apes" story by Edgar Rice Burroughs, F. Scott Fitzgerald's *The Great Gatsby* ("you'd have a decent book if you'd get rid of that Gatsby character") and Gertrude Stein's *The Making of Americans*. (Read a quote from A.C. Fifield's rejection letter to Gertrude Stein in the next chapter.)

And from the film world...

- Rejected by most Hollywood studios ("the worst thing ever written," according to a Columbia TriStar executive), *Pulp Fiction* went on to win the Palme d'Or at Cannes and a best screenwriting Oscar for Roger Avery and Quentin Tarantino.

- Dropping Stephen Spielberg into the director's chair didn't initially help *Raiders of the Lost Ark*, which most studios considered too expensive for a film with no big-name stars attached. *Raiders of the Lost Ark* won five of its nine Oscar nominations and is now considered to be one of the best action-adventure films of all time.

- It took some forty-four rejections before Universal said yes to *Back to the Future*. Other studios had complained that it was either "too family friendly" or "not family friendly enough." Disney was alarmed by allusions to mother-son incest, while Columbia felt it was "not sexual enough." *Back to the Future* was nominated for more than two dozen awards, including four Oscars (it won one) and four Golden Globes. It was the top-grossing film in 1985.

Reading this chapter on your phone? William Orton, president of the Western Union Telegraph Company, turned down Alexander Graham Bell's telephone, calling it an "electrical toy."

♪   ♪   ♪

How do *you* handle rejection? Does it shut you down? Or can you recognize that it's only one person's view? Even if it's a dozen or two or three dozen people who don't like your work, that doesn't mean it's no good. It doesn't even mean it's unpublishable or un-producible. All the rejected writers and titles listed above were ultimately published or produced…and all were ultimately successful. That's equally true for The Beatles and Alexander Graham Bell's "electrical toy."

Don't let other people's judgments influence your discernment about your work. Don't let others' criticisms dam up your flow. Look for ways to nurture your creativity. Find ways to stoke your passion. Remember to trust your story. And keep writing!

When You're Rejected...

I cannot read your M.S. three or four times. Not even one time.
Only one look, only one look is enough.
Hardly one copy would sell here.
Hardly one. Hardly one.
PUBLISHER ARTHUR C. FIFIELD CRUELLY MIMICKING
GERTRUDE STEIN'S STYLE IN HIS 1912 REJECTION LETTER

As you discovered in the previous chapter, Gertrude Stein wasn't the only gifted writer to have experienced rejection. When someone passes on your story, regardless of the reason, here are seven surefire ways to help you get through and past the pain.

1. REAL MEN CRY; REAL WOMEN CRY TOO

Don't bottle up your feelings. And don't get self-destructive. Feel what you feel. All of it. Cry. Curse. Yell. Scream. Throw things. Throw up. Then get past the rejection and move on.

2. CHANNEL YOUR ANGST INTO A CHARACTER

Powerful emotions birth powerful writing. Remember "Rule" #7? Go for your jugular and write all the ways you are feeling into one of your characters — if not as part of this story, then as part of another one.

3. JOURNAL YOUR PAIN

You don't have an available story or character or aren't ready to create one? Journal your disappointment, rage and anguish.

4. TAKE WRITER'S REVENGE

Write a scene where you subject whoever rejected you to something unspeakably hideous, hurtful and horrific. It's the writer's equivalent of sticking pins into a voodoo doll. This scene may never find its way into one of your stories, but you'll have more fun writing it than you ever ought to admit.

5. Look for the Silver Lining

It sounds clichéd, but it remains true: Every experience, however emotionally debilitating, contains within it the seeds of something positive. You may not be able to see the redemptive value of this rejection today, and that's fine. But once the pain has begun to subside, be open to a flash of insight that will reveal the silver lining around your storm cloud of rejection. Need help? Skip ahead to the "See the Perfection in All Things" meditation later in this section.

6. Look for the Spark of Truth

It doesn't happen often, but your rejection letter could include reasons for the turndown, apart from the standard "does not meet our needs at this time." If someone has put in the effort to offer feedback, pay attention to it; use the discernment we talk about in "The Seven Be's of Empowered Feedback" (Section 10) to determine whether it highlights real weaknesses that it would serve you to address in a new draft.

7. Keep Writing

Don't let one rejection — or one hundred or one thousand — stop you. Keep writing and keep seeking ways to become a better writer.

Ask Yourself These Questions When You Have Been Criticized or Rejected

- Can I refuse to let criticism, negative feedback or rejection stop me from moving forward with this or any of my writing projects?
- If I am unable to get an agent, a publishing deal or a screenplay option, can I trust that there may be other reasons why I was called to write this? Can I be okay with that?

EXPLORATION

In your journal, write on the Muse Stream from each of these phrases, going as deep as you dare to discover the extent and impact of your fears.

- When I'm rejected, I...
- My fear of failure...
- My fear of success...
- My fear of others' reactions...
- I trust my story to...

When the Critics Come Knocking...

It's Wednesday evening. I'm about to start on a new draft of this expanded edition of *Writer's Block Unblocked* when I feel a sudden urge to look back over the reviews for the original book. At first, I dismiss the urge. "I'm procrastinating," I mutter as I click on the manuscript file. But then, for no reason I can articulate, I navigate instead to the reviews and start reading.

As they are with all my books, the reviews for *Writer's Block Unblocked* are largely enthusiastic, and it's gratifying to be reminded again of the positive impact my work has. "Maybe I needed this self-confidence boost before diving back in," I say and continue reading.

Then I reach the final review.

It isn't enthusiastic.

Although it's far from scathing, the review is critical enough that my newly boosted self-confidence melts into a pool of judgment and self-doubt, not only about the original edition but about this new one as well. For the rest of the evening and into the next morning, I second-guess every change I have made and worry that everything I'm doing is making *Writer's Block Unblocked* worse rather than better.

Then I remember a merciless review I once got, not for *Writer's Block Unblocked* but for *The MoonQuest*. This review, the worst I have ever received for anything, shredded the plot and my writing...and my morale. After reading it, it was hard to keep believing in myself and my stories.

"For all I teach about how to handle rejection," I wrote at the time, "the criticism still cut deep, still made it difficult for me to continue with my current project. Yet all we can do in the face of others' judgment and our own is to write on."

It took me a few days, but that's what I did.

How? By recognizing that every criticism is only one person's opinion.

By asking why I was giving so much more power to this individual than to the scores of others whose reviews and comments were filled with praise. By reconnecting with the spirit and essence of the story (through meditation and my vision statement), asking it whether any of the criticisms were valid and, most important of all, trusting the answers.

When the answers I got supported my vision over the reviewer's, I had no choice but to trust. "You either trust or you do not," the main character of each of my *Q'ntana* books is told at one point in the story. "There is no halfway in between."

As I reflect on my experience with that *MoonQuest* review, I realize that the situation with *Writer's Block Unblocked* is no different. Why, I ask, am I affording one tepid review more credibility than the many glowing ones? If everything I write and teach is true — about our stories being smarter than we are and knowing themselves better than we do — why am I suddenly mired in self-doubt? If in reconnecting with my vision for the book (and its vision for me), I discern that the criticisms are *not* valid, why am I not trusting the superior wisdom of my book and my Muse?

"You either trust or you do not. There is no halfway in between."

Once again, I have no choice but to trust. I return my focus to the new draft of *Writer's Block Unblocked* and keep going.

Rejection can take many forms: a harsh word, a refusal to publish or produce, poor sales, a bad review. Ultimately, though, the most debilitating rejection comes from within. It happens when we devalue our passion, discredit our intuition, deny our enthusiasm, distrust our Muse and disparage our creativity by abdicating our power to those who criticize us.

I'm not suggesting you ignore all criticism. Some, after all, may include valid points worth noting and learning from. But approach all reviews, the good as well as the bad, from a place of discernment. Don't let yourself be destroyed by the bad reviews. And don't let the good ones pull you from what you know in your heart to be true — about yourself and your work.

Remember "Rule" #11: Empower yourself. This is *your* creative journey. Don't let anyone else take charge of it.

¶ *See also "The Spirit and Essence of Your Story" in Section 12.*

See the Perfection in All Things

A Guided Meditation

Allow 20 to 30 minutes for the experience, longer if you choose to explore those thoughts and feelings in more depth.

Find a quiet place where you won't be disturbed, and get comfortable. Sitting up or lying down; it doesn't matter, as long as you're comfortable. As long as you can leave the rest of the world behind for the next twenty or thirty minutes. Or more.

Are you comfortable? Good. Now, close your eyes. Squeeze them tight and let go. Don't open your eyes when you let go. Keep them shut, but squeeze the tension out. We carry so much tension in our eyes from our computers and mobile devices. From our TVs. From driving. Even from reading books, newspapers and magazines in print. And from the hyper-focus on production and success that is demanded of us so much of the time. So squeeze your eyes tightly again. Let go again. And a third time. And let go again.

Feel yourself relax, even if only a bit. Now, take a deep breath in and let it go. Take another deep breath and let it go. And as you breathe in and out, let your shoulders drop, then drop some more. Feel the tension that you carry in your neck and shoulders, that we all carry, dissolve.

Now, in the same way you squeezed the tension from your eyes, let's squeeze the tension from the rest of your body. Starting from your toes and feet and moving all the way up your body, clench/unclench, stretch and/or flex your muscles, limbs and joints.

Your toes. Your ankles. Your legs. Your glutes. Pull in your stomach and abdomen…and let it go. Stretch your arms and your fingers. Shake out your wrists. Clench and unclench your fists. Hunch up and drop your shoulders. Move your head from left to right and up and down to release the tension in your neck. Grit your teeth and let go. Stretch your mouth as if you're smiling. Open your mouth as wide as you can as if you're yawning. And again, squeeze your eyes tight and release them, keeping them lightly shut.

Now take a deep breath and as you exhale, breathe out any remaining stress from your body, any remaining anxiety from your day. And relax.

It isn't always easy to acknowledge the higher perfection in our lives. "Bad things" happen to all of us. Success, as we have defined it, eludes us. Rejection happens. Criticisms and bad reviews happen. We compare ourselves to others and don't like what we see. Others consider us disappointing in some way, and we feel "less than." When any or all of those things happen, our first impulse, understandably, is to focus on the negative...to shut down. To feel blocked creatively or in some other way.

Yet a higher perfection is always present, whether or not we are able to see it right away. Sometimes, that higher perfection comes in the form of a lesson learned. Sometimes, as a revelation about ourselves, about a current or past situation or about someone or something in our lives. Sometimes, a perceived failure in the moment can be the spark that ignites a later success. Sometimes, a heartbreaking loss can kindle a heart-opening miracle.

Seeing the higher perfection in our lives is not about ignoring hardship, tragedy or bad news. Nor is it about avoiding the intensity of our feelings. Rather, it is about not getting stuck in those feelings, be they feelings of grief, fear, failure, rejection or some form of negativity. It is about feeling what you feel and moving through and past it to see the higher good that is always there. And in those instances when we cannot see or even imagine what that higher good might be, it is about trusting unconditionally in its existence.

So, where in your creative life *in the past* have you felt challenged? Where has someone judged or rejected you or your work? When have those challenges caused you hardship or anxiety? Or fear? Or anger? Or humiliation? Or shame? When have they triggered creative or emotional blocks or shutdowns? It can be something major. It can also be something less important. Something seemingly trivial, even. Let whatever first thought bubbles up into your conscious mind be the one you look at in this moment. You can look at others in other moments, when you repeat this meditation.

Whichever situation or event first enters your awareness, can you now look at it with fresh eyes and an open heart? Can you now see some element of the higher perfection of what occurred? Of what you felt? Of what you experienced?

Take a few moments to be with that, pausing the meditation if necessary. You might even want to stop to write about it in your *Writer's Block Unblocked* journal. Write about what happened and about what you felt at the time. Write about the new ways in which you can now view and perhaps feel gratitude for what happened.

Take all the time you need, and when you're ready, resume the meditation and continue.

Take another deep breath. And another. And another.

Now, where in your *recent or current creative* life are you feeling challenged? Has someone judged or rejected you or your work? Has that caused you hardship or anxiety? Or fear? Or anger? Or humiliation? Or shame? Has it triggered creative or emotional blocks or shutdowns? Again, this can be a major challenge. It can also be something less important. Even something seemingly trivial. Let whatever first thought bubbles up into your conscious mind be the one you look at.

It can be challenging to find the higher perfection in every situation. It can feel impossible. Yet that higher perfection is inevitably present, and that awareness is always available to us when we are open to it.

Take a deep breath and allow yourself to be open to it with regard to whatever recent or current situation came up for you a moment ago. If nothing immediate leapt to mind, what about something from yesterday? Or from last week? Or last month? Go back as far as you need to, but try to keep it as recent as you can.

Take another deep breath. If you feel any tension in your body, breathe it out. Now, let your mind relax and let your heart take over. Let your heart reveal to you some element of good, of higher perfection, in what you are now experiencing or in what you recently experienced. The higher perfection does not have to outweigh the challenge, especially with something current or recent around which you still have strong feelings. But it can take the edge off those strong feelings and, over time, can outweigh them.

Take a few moments to be with that, pausing the meditation if necessary. You might even want to stop to write about it in your *Writer's Block Unblocked* journal. Write about what happened or is happening.

Write your feelings about it. And write about the new ways in which you can now view and perhaps feel gratitude for what happened.

Take all the time you need, and when you're ready, resume the meditation and continue.

Once again, take a few deep breaths in and out, and let yourself slip back into that deeper meditative place.

Don't think about what emerged for you from the past and current experiences you have just revisited. Don't think about what you wrote, if you wrote. Don't think about anything at all. Do your best to focus only on your breath.

As you do, let the time you have spent in this meditation wash over and through you. Allow its transformative energy to anchor itself within you. Allow the new perspectives you have touched to touch other moments and experiences in your creative life...in your life. You needn't know which moments and experiences are being touched or how. Simply allow your new perspective to replace the old one at deep levels, very deep levels.

Sit with that for a few moments more. Pause the meditation if you need extra time, resuming when you are ready.

When you do feel ready, slowly return your awareness to your body... to whatever is supporting you as you are sitting or lying down...to any sounds coming from inside the room or outside it.

Wiggle your fingers and toes. Move your head gently from left to right, then back. Move your feet. Do whatever it takes to ground you back into the present, physically. And when you're ready, open your eyes. Sit or lie quietly for a few minutes longer before getting up.

Note any further thoughts in your *Writer's Block Unblocked* journal, then get up and get on with your day, knowing that something fundamental has shifted within you.

12. Be the Writer You Are

We are the music makers,
And we are the dreamers of dreams...
ARTHUR WILLIAM EDGAR O'SHAUGHNESSY

A man who wants to lead the orchestra
must turn his back on the crowd.
JAMES CROOK

Acts of Commitment

What does commitment mean? It means making writing a priority in your life. It means not letting fear, excuses, procrastination or distractions divert you from listening for the voice of your Muse and surrendering to the call of your story or stories. It means letting the ideas of your heart find expression through your mind. It means trusting that your story knows the way and trusting it to guide you from first page to last. It means honoring your passion and respecting yourself.

It means committing to *you* as the writer you are.

Exploration

Ask yourself this questions and don't think about the answer. Let it emerge freely and honestly...on the Muse Stream, where appropriate:

- What steps can I take, today, to strengthen my commitment to my writing, to my stories, to my creativity, to my passion? To myself?

The Gift of Your Words

Among your many gifts, if you are reading this today, is a gift to create... an ability to communicate, to weave worlds of wonder with your words.

Of course, you possess that gift. We all do. But you have chosen to let that gift possess you. You have chosen to allow the voice of your Muse free access to your heart and mind. You wouldn't be here — in this book, on this page — were that not so.

How are you giving that gift today? How are you honoring your gift, your Muse? If you haven't yet, take a moment — today, now — to give the gift of your passion, to free the voice of your Muse onto the page and into the world.

Heartful Acts of Revolution

Perhaps you will be judged for what you write. Not everyone's heart is as open as yours, perhaps. But everyone's sings the same song.

Thus, the fiercest ridicule and loudest judgment will come from those who are touched most deeply by your words. That's right. The fiercest ridicule and loudest, cruelest judgment will come from those who are touched most deeply by your words. Let me say that one more time, for it is a radical thought.

> *The fiercest ridicule and loudest, cruelest judgment will come from those who are touched most deeply by your words.*

How is that possible? It's simple. Your critics are touched at a place deeper than they feel comfortable going, so their reaction and response is one of cruelty.

Their cruelty is not directed at you, though their minds and yours might think that. Their cruelty is directed toward themselves. It is themselves they would judge but cannot, dare not. So they direct their judgment outward, toward you.

Let it roll off you. Let it not matter. For it does not. No word that anyone can say to you — be it in love or fear — can or should alter the truth of your heart. Nor should it alter the truth of your path.

Walk gently on that path, but speak — and write — from a place of strength.

Your most potent place of strength is your heart. Your heart is in touch with everyone and everything that is, was or ever will be. Your heart knows all.

That is why it is so important to listen to your heart and trust in its truth. For all the truth that is, was or ever will be resides there. And as you touch that place, as you feel that place, as you are that place, your words will fill hearts, topple kingdoms and make whole what has been ripped apart — wherever they are read, whispered or sung.

That is the power of your heart. That is the power of your words.

Write from your heart. Write from your heart with courage and love. Write from your heart as though nothing else mattered, and your words will be acts of revolution that transform worlds.

If you can't touch that place today, you will touch it tomorrow and more fully still the day after that.

For there may be walls upon walls upon walls, topped with barbed wire and broken glass and guarded by monsters, demons and trolls, that encircle your heart and block your words. They may have been built up over years, over decades...over lifetimes, if you believe in reincarnation.

Those walls have no power.

They can collapse in an instant. And in that same instant, all those monsters will turn out to be as tame and as loving as kittens...if you show them that there is no need to be cruel.

Everything is already there, already in place. All the stories, all the scripts, all the essays, all the songs, all the poems, all the books, all the healings, all the words are there, in the right order. Simply tune your inner radio dial to K-HEART and all you require will appear without delay.

For there is no time. There is only now, only this word...now this one...and now this one.

Then, before you know it you're done and kingdoms have toppled, demons are licking your face and the world has changed, for you have changed.

And next time, it will be easier.

Try This

When you choose to allow the voice of your Muse free access to your heart and mind, writing becomes a revolutionary act, one that transforms you and, through you, the world...one that, through the simple act of surrendering to your passion, helps cocreate a better world.

Now, right now, commit an act of revolution. Write. Write anything, but write it from your heart. Write it from your heart, without judgment. And know that nothing will ever be the same again.

¶ *See also the "Write from Your Heart" meditation in Section 13.*

Say What?

It's common for writers to complain, "I can't write" or "I'm blocked" or "I have writer's block." But ask yourself this: What are you owning about yourself and your writing when you use phrases like that? What are you reinforcing?

Without censoring yourself, pay attention to your language. Not the language you write. The language you speak. Listen for the words and phrases that reveal — sometimes subtly, sometimes with alarming clarity — what it is you feel, what it is you fear, what it is you judge.

Here's a selection of words and phrases to watch for...and learn from.

- ✓ **Block** or **Blocked** — *As in, "I have writer's block" or "I'm blocked."* You don't and you're not.

- ✓ **Impossible** — *Any use, unless preceded by the word "not."* You are an innately creative being of infinite potential. Nothing is impossible.

- ✓ **I'm Not** — *As in, "I'm not creative" or "I'm not talented."* Any "I'm not" negates a part of you. Replace your I'm not's with I am's, and let each "I am" be a declaration of empowerment that braces, bolsters and buttresses your self-esteem, your creativity and your creative enterprises.

- ✓ **Hard** or **Difficult** or **Challenging** — *As in, "It's hard because..." or "It's difficult to..." or "It's challenging to..."* Give no energy to negativity or perceived difficulty. Just do it.

- ✓ **Pointless** or **Futile** or **Waste** — *As in, "What I'm writing is pointless" or "This is futile" or "This is a waste of time/effort."* There is no such thing as a wasted word, phrase, sentence, draft, manuscript or script. Every word, phrase, sentence, draft and manuscript or script you write is part of the creative journey that carries you to the next, and to the next one after that.

- ✓ **Just** or **Only** — *As in, "This is just a journal entry" or "This is just a first* draft" or "This is just for me" or "I've written only five hundred words" or fifty or five... Don't belittle your achievements. Celebrate every milestone, regardless of how small it seems to your critical mind.

- ✓ **Control** — *As in, "I need to be in control of this story or character" or "I have to control this process."* Abandon control. You're not in charge, and any thoughts that you might be are illusion...or delusion.

- ✓ **Has to Be** — *As in, "This has to be a poem" or "This has to be a screenplay" or "This has to be a thriller" or "This has to be a full-length novel."* Your story knows its length and form...its genre...its medium. Trust it.

- ✓ **Order** or **Sequence** — *As in, "I need to write this in order" or "I can't write scenes, chapters or sections out of sequence."* Surrender to the superior wisdom of your story and let it emerge as it chooses to emerge, not as you would have it emerge.

- ✓ **Trying** — *As in, "I'm trying to make time to write" or "I'm trying to write every day."* To quote Yoda: "Do or do not. There is no try." Set goals you *know* you can meet, and meet them.

- ✓ **Not Enough** — *As in, "not good enough" or "not creative enough" or "not enough time."* There is always enough, and you are always enough. Period. Don't subscribe to lack in any aspect of your life. Embrace abundance and the abundant, and embrace the abundantly creative being that you are.

- ✓ **Not As Good As** — *As in, "I'll never be as good as..." or "What I wrote is not as good as what Janet or Joe (or Shakespeare or Stephen King or Joan Didion or Margaret Atwood or anyone else) wrote."* You don't have to write like that. Somebody already has. The world isn't waiting for another Shakespeare, Stephen King, Joan Didion or Margaret Atwood. The world waits for you. You and your unique expression. You and your words. You and your story. Comparison is nothing more than an excuse to put yourself down. Celebrate who you are and where you are. Read the masters. Learn from the masters. Then be the master *you* are.

- ✓ **Can't** or **Cannot** or **Don't Dare** — *As in, "I can't write" or "I can't write well" or "I can't write now" or "I can't write/say that" or "I don't* *dare write/say that."* There is nothing you cannot or dare not write, say, do or be. Stop judging yourself. Stop limiting yourself. Start being yourself.

- ✓ **Problem** — *In any context.* There is no problem in your writing or anywhere else in your life that does not carry within it the seeds of opportunity. Even if the opportunity seems invisible in the moment, trust in its existence and shift your focus from the apparent negative to the always-present potential for a redemptive outcome.

- ✓ **Supposed to** *or* **Have to** *or* **Must** *or* **Must Not** — *In any context.* Where do your "supposed to's," "have to's" and "must not's" come from? A teacher? A parent? A spouse? A sibling? A friend? A boss? A colleague? Another writer? Don't look outside yourself for guidance or validation. Go within. Listen to your heart. Listen to your story. Listen to your Muse. Listen to the infinite mind that holds within it the wisdom of the universe and that lives within you, always.

- ✓ **Should** — *In any context.* Have you ever noticed that the word "shoulder" begins with the word "should"? Have you ever noticed how much tension you carry in your shoulders? Un-should yourself and feel the burdens that you have allowed others to place on your shoulders melt away.

Now, focus instead on some of these words and phrases...

- ✓ **Surrender** — Can you surrender to the story you are writing? To the creative imperative that underlies it? Can you surrender to your Muse? To the stories it would have you write?

- ✓ **Release** *and* **Let Go** — Can you let go all thoughts that limit you and hold you back? Can you release the reins on your creativity? On your life?

- ✓ **Fly Free** *and* **Unlimited** — Can you let yourself fly free? Can you begin to see your potential as unlimited?

- ✓ **Leap of Faith** — Every blank page represents a leap of faith. How about taking one of those leaps, right/write now?

How about *trust*? Or *allow*? Or *I can*? Or *I will*? Or *I am*? How about *possible* or *doable* or *now*?

How about focusing on what you have accomplished, not on what is lacking from your work? How about reminding yourself that you are a writer...and a powerful one? How about remembering that everything is not only possible, but as easy as you will allow it to be?

As you do that, you will birth more creative excellence than you could ever produce by worrying, judging, diminishing and deriding whatever random writings, musings and jottings first issue from your pen or keyboard.

Listen to your words. Hear what they tell you about what you think and believe. Then begin to transform those thoughts and beliefs by choosing new words.

TRY THIS

Are there words or phrases not on the list that you use about yourself or about your work that are limiting, judging or diminishing? As you move through your day, be more conscious of what you're speaking and thinking. *Gently and lovingly* correct yourself when those words or thoughts are critical, demeaning or unsupportive — of yourself or of others — or when they deny you your infinite potential, your innate creativity or your inner vision. Let your words be your teachers, and learn from them.

When Was the Last Time You Told Your Story?

Computer scientist/theologian Anne Foerst suggests that we call ourselves *Homo narrandus* ("storytelling man") instead of *Homo sapiens* ("wise man"). That's because storytelling is innate, possibly predating spoken language. It's easy to imagine that after our cave-dweller ancestors returned to the communal fire from a day's hunting and gathering, they gestured, grunted and mimed their adventures to their fellow primitives. One way or another, we have been telling stories ever since.

We are all natural storytellers. Nearly everything we communicate, whether it's a casual watercooler chat or a deep conversation with a close friend, is some form of story.

Too often, though, our stories are censored...even from ourselves. Too often, we live safe and small, reining in our passions, opening to none but the least risky experiences, sharing only the most superficial aspects of our lives.

We have been conditioned to be afraid of opening our hearts and expressing our depth. We have been taught to be shallow and clever. We have learned to equate vulnerability with unacceptable risk.

And we wonder why our creativity is stifled and our self-expression muted.

Yet the only way to touch others deeply is to allow ourselves to be touched deeply. And the only way to tell the stories that change lives, including our own, is through the kinds of leaps of faith that open us to judgment, mockery and ridicule...those same leaps of faith that open us to profound connection and transformation, to the ever-present magic and miracle that wait only for us to notice them and welcome them into our lives.

My novel *The MoonQuest* is the story of a world where storytelling has been banned, storytellers have been banished and all vision and creativity have been extinguished.

Not surprisingly, it is also my story.

I don't remember why, when or how my storytelling was silenced. All I know is that I was dead inside until *The MoonQuest* began to tell itself through me. As its main characters found their voices, I found mine. As they discovered and shared their darkness, I discovered and shared mine. Only then did I realize that *The MoonQuest*'s story of creative awakening was also mine, that it was a story I *had* to free into the world — for me as much as for anyone else.

From that story came other stories. From that opening came other openings. From that healing came other healings.

As I write in the epigraph to *The Voice of the Muse*, writing is "truly a tool of wizards, witches and sorcerers." It's through the alchemy of our stories, lived authentically and shared truthfully, that all worlds change, beginning with our own.

When was the last time you told *your* story — honestly, vulnerably, courageously?

Whether it was last night or last year, it's time to do it again — to deepen the experience, for yourself and for all those fortunate enough to share in it.

Try This

What story are you carrying inside you that is yearning to be freed onto the page? What story are you carrying inside you that, once freed onto the page, will also free you? Now is the time to listen to its call and start freeing it onto the page. You're not sure how? Start with one word, any word. Then, surrendering unconditionally to your story, add another and another. Then another. Don't think about what the story is or where it's taking you. Don't struggle for the right word, right character or right plot, right theme or right idea. Just start, follow that free-flowing river of creativity I call the Muse Stream, and trust in the journey...the journey to worlds beyond your conscious imagination.

The Spirit and Essence of Your Story

A Guided Meditation

Allow at least 35 minutes for this meditation and for the writing experience that flows from it.

Get comfortable and close your eyes. Take a deep breath in, and let it go. Take another. Let that go. As you breathe in and out, let your shoulders drop and feel the muscles in your arms and neck relax. Feel your whole body relax.

With each inhalation, breathe in more deeply and feel yourself breathing in to the essence of your story, to the essence of your creativity, to the essence of your creative power, to the powerful essence of you.

And with each exhalation, feel more and more of the tension dissolve from your body. Feel the anxiety dissolve from your body. Feel the emotional strain and stress dissolve from your body. Let your shoulders drop some more, and feel only peace and calm envelop you.

Be in the moment with that peace. Be in the moment with your breath. Be one with your breath, so that the only thing you are aware of in this instant is this instant...is the essence of this instant and, within that essence of the moment, the essence of your story, a story that has called to you so strongly for so long...a story whose call you now, finally, feel ready to answer.

Remember, "story" is not limited to fiction, nor is it limited to a book or script. "Story" transcends form, medium and genre to include anything and everything that you find yourself writing or being called to write...or being afraid to write.

So, what is this story?

It is the story that you may have felt unable to write. Until now. It is the story that already exists whole and complete in its own invisible realm. It's the story that waits for you to engage with it, that waits for you to trust it. That waits for you to surrender to it. Unconditionally.

So, acknowledge that your story knows itself better than you do. Acknowledge that and open to all that that story has to offer you now through this experience.

Continue to focus on your breath...to go deep within. As you do, as you let your breath carry you deep into your heart and deep in the heart of your story, allow an image, any image, to bubble up into your conscious awareness, an image that represents the energy of your story.

This image need not make conventional sense. There's a good chance it won't. The image could be a thing. It could be a color. It could be a person. It could be an animal. It could be a sound. It could be a feeling.

Whatever it is, let it bubble up into your awareness. Don't judge it. Don't censor it. Let it emerge and, whatever it is, be okay with it. Go with first thoughts. Always go with first thoughts.

Be aware, too, that if this is a repeat meditative experience with this same story, a different image may emerge for you now than emerged last time. That's okay. Go with whatever bubbles up for you today. Again, first thoughts.

We are dealing with a nonphysical energy and with your mind's representation of that energy. We are also dealing with your evolving relationship with your story. It's natural for your imagery to evolve as well.

Trust today's first-thoughts representation of that energy. Trust tomorrow's too, if it shows up differently. Trust that whatever emerges whenever it emerges is perfect for who you are in the moment you intuit and discern it.

Now, before you begin to converse or connect with that image, if you haven't already, get a sensory sense of it. Use your senses to help you connect more fully and deeply with that essence, with that energy — with the essence and energy of your story — through the image that has emerged for you today.

Get a sense of color, if there's color. Of shape, if there's shape. Of depth, if there's depth. Of texture, if there's texture.

Which other of your senses is awakened by it? Smell? Taste? Sound? Music, perhaps? Emotions?

As always, don't second-guess what shows up. Don't try to change what shows up. Remember: It's all about first thoughts. Always.

Not all your physical and emotional senses may apply to this image, but they may. Or those that are not relevant today may be relevant on a different day, or in a different, perhaps unconventional way.

So what does this image look like to you right now, even as you know that it could change in the next moment? What does it feel like? If it feels powerful, don't let yourself feel overwhelmed by that power. Know that that power is you, and that that power is an expression not only of your story's essence, but of your essence. Not only of the story you are or will be writing, but of *your* story.

Whatever this image is, however you perceive it, whatever its qualities and characteristics, embrace it. Take it in. Breathe it in. Fully. And let your sensory and emotional experience of this image connect you more intimately than ever before with the energy and essence of the story it represents.

It's time now to listen, to listen to that image, whatever it is. It's time to listen from a deep place deep within you, to listen with your heart to what your story, through this image, has to tell you. You might not hear a conscious message, but something will move through you, however unconsciously. Trust that. And trust that however you experience it is the right and perfect way for you right now.

So take a few moments to listen...

Now that you have heard, felt or sensed whatever you have heard, felt or sensed, it's time to ask a question of your story through the intermediary of this image. So silently ask a question.

It could be a question about the story's ideas, themes, contents, plot, characters, arguments or general thrust. It could be a question about your reluctance to engage with it. It could be a question about its fate. It could be a question about its value — to you or to the world. There is no right or wrong question.

Once you have asked your question, wait silently for an answer.

You may hear an answer right away. You may sense your answer. You may get nothing clear or obvious. Even if your question seems unanswered in this moment, an answer will come in another moment, likely in an unexpected way in an unexpected moment.

Trust that. And trust whatever comes first.

Ask another question and listen for another answer. And another.

Before we complete this experience, your story has some reassurance to offer you. Perhaps it's related to your questions. Perhaps it related to some of the ways you have felt stuck or blocked in your creative expression. Perhaps it's something else. Whatever it is, listen for it, and hear or feel it in whatever way you hear or feel it.

Finally, let your story offer you some closing words, whichever words come, to help you move forward on the next step of your creative journey with it.

Listen for those.

Remember that you have been chosen to bring this story into the physical in the form of words on a page or screen. Whatever that may feel like in some moments, that is one of the greatest gifts of your life. Be with that for a moment or two. And feel what that feels like.

Now once again, be conscious of your breath. Be conscious, too, that this process will not end when you open your eyes, but that the intuitive sensings and messages will continue in the hours, days and weeks ahead. Remain open to them. Remain available to them. Trust them.

Be aware now of your physical body, of the physical space you now occupy, as you let your breath return you to full awareness. And when you feel ready, taking all the time you need, gently open your eyes and be fully present, ready to jot down any notes or thoughts from this meditative journey you have just traveled.

13. The Courage to Create

> Creativity takes courage.
> HENRI MATISSE

> The role of the writer is not to say what we all can say,
> but what we are unable to say.
> ANAÏS NIN

Write to Connect

The call to write is a call to share our emotional depth with others. It's a call to be vulnerable. It's a call to connect.

Thing is, we rarely touch others at a deep level when we connect mind-to-mind, though that connection is a powerful and important one. We touch others at a deep level when we connect heart-to-heart.

Unless we write from our deepest heart, unless we tell the stories that move us, we will never move our readers.

I spent the first chunk of my writing career avoiding writing from the inside-out. Instead, I observed and reported, intellectually and dispassionately. I told stories, but without heart. I wrote only from the outside.

In not revealing my feelings — oftentimes, not even to myself — I failed to engage my readers in any but superficial ways. I failed them and I failed myself.

I didn't connect. I didn't connect with them because I couldn't connect within myself.

Do you want to write truth, the truth from which powerful fiction and nonfiction arise? If you want to write truth, if you want to write words that will touch the deepest emotions and connections and truths of your reader, then you must write what your heart calls on you to write. You must go where you have never dared go before — in your writing, certainly; in your life, perhaps. You must feel and write your passion.

You must, as I write in "Rule" #7, be vulnerable and write from a place of powerful emotion, especially the one you would prefer not to write about. The good news is that once you commit that emotion to paper, you strip it of its power over you and free it to empower your work.

You free it, as well, to empower your readers. You empower them to feel their emotions, to be vulnerable and to share their stories.

"We tell our stories in order to live," Joan Didion wrote.

We tell our stories, too, to connect.

Exploration

Ask yourself these questions in your *Writer's Block Unblocked* journal, but don't think about the answers. And don't feel you have to answer each question independently if that doesn't feel right.

Let your individual answers (or whatever single answer these questions trigger) emerge freely and honestly, writing them on the Muse Stream in a free-flowing, stream-of-consciousness way where appropriate. Let yourself be surprised by the answers.

- Where am I refusing to be vulnerable in my writing?
- Where am I afraid to reveal my feelings, perhaps even to myself?
- In what ways am I reluctant to connect, heart-to-heart, with my readers?
- Where, right now, can I go for the jugular — *my* jugular — and dare to write from my emotional epicenter?

Write from the Heart

A Guided Meditation

Allow at least 30 minutes for this meditation and for the writing experience that flows from it.

My studio recording of this meditation is available for download or streaming as part "The Voice of the Muse Companion: Guided Meditations for Writers." See "Guided Meditations" in Section 1 ("Getting Started") to find out how to access the recording, as well as for tips on how best to use this book's meditations.

Relax. Close your eyes. Focus on your breath. Breathe deeply. In and out. In and out. In and out. Continue to breathe, in and out, breathing in relaxation, breathing in freedom…allowing any stress, anxiety or tightness to relax into freedom on your breath.

Listen to the rhythm of your heart. Feel it beating. Feel it pumping life throughout your body. Down into your abdomen, groin, legs, feet and toes. Up into your neck and shoulders, your mouth, nose and ears. Your eyes. Feel its power in your arms, hands and fingers. The hands you write with.

The hands of creation.

Feel that life force circulate freely, spiraling throughout your body, creating patterns and shapes, colors and sounds.

Listen to the rhythm of that life force that is centered in your heart. And in that rhythm, through that rhythm, listen for the voice of your Muse.

What does it mean to write from the heart? Is it physically possible? Can your fingers reach back in on themselves, travel up your arms, past your elbows and shoulders, then down your chest to touch that central mind that, were it truly in charge, would revolutionize your writing and your life?

For, yes, your heart is your central mind — a mind more powerful, life-fulfilling and life-affirming than your brain, as powerful and magical a piece of machinery as that is.

Yet that's what it is: a piece of machinery. A wondrous, miraculous machine, but a machine nonetheless.

When we let machines do our writing for us, when we let machines do our living for us, the result is mechanical, soulless and spiritless.

We don't touch others at a deep level when we connect mind-to-mind, though that connection is a powerful and important one. We touch others at a deep level when we connect heart-to-heart.

So let your fingers reach back in on themselves. See them traveling through your arms...on the inside, not the outside.

See them reaching past your wrists and up your forearms, past your elbows and up to your shoulders. Let them stop there for a moment, and from their place deep inside your muscles, bone and tissue, massage and caress the tension from, in and around those shoulders.

Feel the release as your fingers press deeply into the soul of your shoulder, releasing all the stress, all the fear, all the tightness, all the anxiety, all the "shoulds."

Notice the word "should." See it write itself out in your mind's eye, and see that this word "should" forms seventy-five percent of the word "shoulder."

It's in our shoulders that we hold all our shoulds. And it's from our shoulders that our shoulds must be released.

Now is the time to massage those shoulds away. Now is the time to un-should-er and feel the lightness return to your shoulders, to your entire body.

Now is the time to let the burden drop from your shoulders. Now is the time to unshoulder all you have been bearing. All the responsibility. All the obligations. All the weight. All the burdens of this time and all time.

Feel your fingers massage them away...out of your shoulders and out of your neck. Let the shoulds dissolve: "I should write about this"; "I should write this way"; "I should be careful not to offend"; "I should be doing this or that instead of writing"; "I should be writing instead of doing this or that."

Let those shoulds and all shoulds melt under your touch. Let that sense of lightness and freedom you were born with return, if only for a moment.

Once you feel the return of some of your natural lightness, once you feel some of that un-should-ering, let your fingers continue down to your heart — the organ on the left side of your chest and the chakra or energy center in the middle of your chest.

Let your fingers continue down, and as they do, let them clear away any cobwebs, let them unlock any doors, gates or walls, let them move in gently and caress that place of love with love. Let the energy of that love, that aloha, of that place of heart-centeredness, fill your fingertips.

Let the memory of all the love you have experienced, all the loving experiences you have lived, let that memory fill your fingertips so that when, in a few moments, you return them to the keyboard or pen, that love will infuse every letter and word that flows from them, from that connection to your heart that is always there and can always be reignited.

Continue to breathe, to breathe deeply, as you open your heart and clear away and free all that has been scarred, barricaded and bottled up. Breathe in the clarity. Breathe in the focus. Breathe in the love, the self-love, the love of your heart, your Muse, your words. Breathe in the aloha.

Continue to breathe, in and out, in and out, for a few more moments.

In and out.

In and out.

In and out.

Slowly.

Deeply.

Fully.

As you breathe, listen. Focus your attention on your heart. Focus all your attention on your heart. In this moment, let nothing exist but your heart.

Listen to it. Listen for its voice, for the voice of your Muse as expressed through your heart. Listen to your heart. Still yourself and listen.

Your heart has a message for you. A word, a phrase...many words, many phrases. As you continue to focus and listen, you will hear it. Clearly.

Once you hear it, write what you hear.

Continue listening and writing, listening and writing, recording all that you hear or sense, in this moment.

And now this one.

And now this one.

If you hear or sense nothing at this time, don't judge yourself. Simply launch your journey using this key phrase: "My heart speaks to me of..."

In either case, write on the Muse Stream, remembering to keep your pen moving across the page or your fingers dancing across the keyboard, letting it be the medium through which your heart words speak to you.

Write your heart words until you sense completion.

Then hold the silence for a few moments longer, open to anything new your heart has to say.

Living the Creative Life

You can choose to walk away from writer's block. You can't choose to walk away from whatever is causing it. That's because the same precepts that can guide us to more creative, imaginative, expressive, passion-filled, spontaneous and free-flowing writing and artistry apply equally to living a more creative, imaginative, expressive, passion-filled and spontaneous life. And what blocks us in one is certain to block us in the other.

That's why the 12½ "Rules" for Living a Creative Life that follow largely parallel the 12½ "Rules" for Freeing Up Your Creative Flow you experienced in Section 4.

12½ "Rules" for Living a Creative Life

It's February 2007 and my optometrist has just finished telling me that my eye strain is the result not, as I feared, of deteriorating vision. Rather, my eyesight has improved since my last checkup, and my glasses are now uncomfortably strong. While this isn't the first time my vision has strengthened between appointments, it's the first time the improvement hasn't resulted from a regime of meditation and eye exercises.

"I sat in my car after the appointment," I write in *Acts of Surrender*, "and pondered the question as a rare Southern California rain splattered noisily on my windshield. Could it be that what I am trumps what I do? Could eye exercises and meditation matter less than the spirit and philosophy that underlie them? If that were true, could a life lived in surrender to the infinite wisdom of an infinite mind produce health benefits equal to more accepted methods? My life suggested to me that it could: I hadn't been to a doctor in nearly a decade, nor had I suffered anything more than the occasional cold or mild flu. People even told me that I looked younger. I thought back to the 'rules' for writing that I had crafted a few years before for an early ebook version of *The Voice of the Muse* and wondered whether I could apply them to life. I pulled out my computer, looked up the originals and realized that, with minor modifications, I could, easily. I adapted them on the spot."

Like my "rules" for writing, my "rules" for living continue to evolve. Here is the latest iteration...

1. There Are No Rules

How can there be rules when, at their most fulfilling, both creativity and life are all about innovation — about blazing your own trail, breaking new ground, breaking old rules? Living a creative life means there can never be a single right way that works for everyone all the time. There is no universal wrong way either, only the way that works for you *today*.

2. Listen to Your Heart

Your heart speaks with the voice of God (or whatever you call that divine/creative/infinite intelligence we all carry within us). Listen and trust that intuitive voice with neither judgment nor censorship. It's wiser than you are and knows, better than you ever will, both the story you're living and the story you're writing. Always align your mind to the wisdom of your heart. Let that voice guide you — as you write and as you live.

3. Embrace Imperfection

In your life's endeavors as in your creative endeavors, strive for excellence, which is achievable, not for perfection, which isn't.

4. Trust Your Intuition

Your intuition often shows up in the form of "first thoughts." Second thoughts are nearly always judgmental, self-censoring thoughts. Trust what you feel and what you sense, and don't get caught up in conventional logic or conventional wisdom, which is inevitably more conventional than wise.

5. Surrender

You're not in charge, so abandon control, get out of the way and let your story have its way with you — the story you are living as much as the story you are writing.

6. Be in the Moment

What works for you today may not work tomorrow or ever again, so you might as well live in the present moment. Focus on now — on the breath you are breathing and the word you are writing. The next will always come if you don't worry about it...if you surrender to it.

7. Be Vulnerable

Share your pain and your passion — as you live and in your writing. That's what makes you human. That's what connects you with others, in your life and in your art. Or, as I put it in *Dialogues with the Divine*, "Walk the earth naked, clothed only in your truth."

8. Love Yourself and Your Words

Treat yourself and everything you create as you would your child or best friend: with love, compassion and respect. Don't beat yourself up, and don't demean or denigrate yourself or your work, for any reason.

9. Strip Off Your Straitjackets

Don't live or write according to others' expectations...or according to your preconceptions. Free yourself to follow the path that is uniquely yours. Free your words to take on the form that is uniquely theirs. Surrender to the resulting gifts and let yourself be amazed and awed by them.

10. Commit to Your Passion

Find your passion and embrace it. Passionately. Then commit to your passion, unconditionally. Whatever it is and however you define it, be it. Leap into it with every cell. Immerse yourself into it with every drop of blood that flows through your veins. Let your passion inform every choice, every decision, every step, every word.

11. Abandon Ruts and Rote

Kick free of your ruts. Ditch your routines. If you're feeling stuck, shake things up a bit. Make different choices. If you're afraid that you will make a "wrong" choice, stop worrying and make *any* choice. In your writing, write something, *anything*, to get started or to keep going. Find ways to keep moving with the current of life and to keep flowing in the stream of creation.

12. Empower Yourself

This is your life and your creative journey. Don't let anyone else take charge of them. Don't let anyone else tell you how to live and express them (or how not to live and express them). Empower yourself by defining success on your terms, not on anyone else's. Then set easy goals and meet them. In doing so, you will set yourself up for success, not for failure — as you live and as you write.

12½. There Are No Rules

There are no rules. None. Never. So lighten up and stop taking your life (and your art) so seriously. Have fun as you create and as you live.

♪ ♪ ♪

Do I live these perfectly? Of course not (see "Rule" #3). But to the best of my imperfect ability in each moment, I live as authentically as I can, surrendering as unconditionally as I am able to the truest path I can envision, honoring my passion with each choice and focusing on what I have, not on what I lack. I write the same way.

Try This

Use each of these rules as a kickoff to a Muse Stream writing exercise. See where these free-flows take you. See what they tell you — about your writing and about your life.

Exploration 1

A blockage is a blockage is a blockage. If your creativity is choked and stifled, then a corresponding area of your life must be equally stuck. It cannot be otherwise.

Ask yourself these questions in your *Writer's Block Unblocked* journal, but don't think about the answers. And don't feel you have to answer each question independently if that doesn't feel right.

Let your individual answers (or whatever single answer these questions trigger) emerge freely and honestly, writing them on the Muse Stream in a free-flowing, stream-of-consciousness way where appropriate. Let yourself be surprised by the answers.

- Where is my personal, professional or emotional life not flowing?
- Where have my creativity issues spilled over into the rest of my life?
- How have my life issues affected my creativity?

Exploration 11

When you free up your life blocks, the corresponding barriers to your creativity will also start to dissolve. When you release the choke hold on your writing, your personal life will also open up.

Write about the connections you are aware of between your life and your creativity. Use the "rules" for writing and living, if that's helpful. Then, on the Muse Stream, explore those connections that lie beneath your conscious awareness and see what you discover. And see what, through your discoveries, you can begin to transform — in your writing and in your life.

Remember Who You Are

Who are you? You are more than a mass of skin, bone, muscle and sinew. More than the blood pumping through your heart and coursing through your veins. More than the breath that flows into your lungs and out again. More than all the cells that unite to shape your physical body.

You are more than your brain's incomparable power to reason, compute, calculate and recall. More than its immeasurable ability to amass, assess, organize and analyze.

You are stronger than the most muscular of machines, more resilient than the most elastic of rubbers, more powerful than the most formidable of turbines.

You are greater than the sum of your emotions. Greater, certainly, than your fear. You are passion and compassion. You are generosity and benevolence. You are boundless courage. You are love without limit. You are a miracle of heart and soul.

You are untold stories waiting for the storyteller you are to free them into form, through the writing of them and the living of them.

You are a human being who too easily forgets all that. So take a moment, now, to remember that…to remember all that you are.

Resistance is Futile

Resistance is futile. You seek to hide. There is no hiding. You seek to escape. There is no escape.

There is only your truth. There is only your heart. And although you can try to hide from them, you can't escape, for they will follow you to the ends of the earth and will ultimately have their way with you.

So why not surrender — now? The pain is in the resistance. The so-called writer's block is in the resistance.

Writer's block is nothing more nor less than your resistance to those words that would have their way with you if you would but surrender to them. Instead, you say, "No, not these words. I want others."

Well, there are no other words. There are only heart words.

If you would but open your heart and allow what longs to flow from you easy egress, there would be no block. If you would but make your fear subservient to your courage, there would be no block. For fear and courage can coexist, but not as equals. One must take precedence.

Fear leads to inaction. Courage to action. Fear and courage evenly matched lead to paralysis, which is the same as inaction.

So, still your judge. Just for this moment. Now for this one. Now for this one. And now for this one. And maybe, now, for this one too.

Still that part of yourself that would judge you, your words or both to be unworthy, silly, without merit, laughable. Still that part of yourself that fears being opened to ridicule...or worse.

Nothing will happen to you for putting words on a page. No one can harm you, no matter how outrageous your words or thoughts, for what flows from you onto the page.

Ah, but I hear you say, "I don't want to see myself saying, thinking, writing...believing those words that want to get onto the page."

That's a different matter, one you must face.

Perhaps that is where the fear comes from, a fear you may not understand or know you possess.

Perhaps.

If it be so, then know that when you accept the call to write, you accept the call to change your life.

The mere act of sitting in silence in front of a blank page or screen is a life-changing and life-affirming experience. The mere presence of that vacuum, which you have created and are trusting your Muse to fill, is a life-changing experience.

Let me repeat that: The mere act of sitting down to write is a life-changing experience.

So why would it come as a surprise to discover that the words themselves will change you?

Why do we write? To discover what we believe, what we know, who we are. Just as we live, day to day, moment to moment, to discover those things. If it is change you fear, then you will face writer's block. Stopping the flow of change-words stops the flow of all words.

What is it you fear? That you will discover what you think or believe? That setting those thoughts or beliefs to paper is an unbreakable commitment to them?

Nothing you think or believe in this moment is fixed for all time. It is true in this moment alone. It may still be true in the next, or it may not be. Do not be afraid of change — in your writing or in yourself. Let each moment be a lifetime, complete in itself, as each word is. Live it fully, and then move on to the next, knowing that, in the next moment, your story, your life or both could change beyond recognition.

Let that lifetime unfold when it will. For now, be in this moment, with its unfolding words, thoughts and beliefs. For now, let your resistance dissolve on the Muse Stream of creativity.

You possess the courage...the courage to create.

Write, Now

Too many books, classes and workshops insist that you must know what your story is about before you start writing. Some even insist that you outline it ahead of time. They're wrong. You don't have to know what your story is about before you start writing. You don't have to know anything about its theme, thrust or plot in order to begin. All you have to do is begin. All you have to do is write one word, then another, then another. Then another, all the way to the end.

As you do that, in surrender to the word of the moment and in surrender to the superior wisdom of your story, the story you think you know nothing about will reveal itself to you.

So pick a word. Any word. Let it be the first random word that comes to mind, or the first word your eyes light on as you glance around the room. Or flip to a page in this or any book, close your eyes and let your finger blindly search out the word that will launch your writing.

Don't second-guess the word that emerges. Don't discard your word and try again if you don't like what your mind or finger has come up with. Don't dismiss even the most unexceptional of words, even something as innocuous as "a" or "the" or "of" or "and" or "but." Your story in its wisdom, chose this word. Your job is to surrender to it.

Now, take a few deep breaths into your word. Embody that word.

Fill yourself with that word, and fill that word with all of you.

Write the word.

Without stopping to think about it, let another word follow that one. And another. And another.

What about sentences and paragraphs? What about a subject?

You are the subject. I don't mean you will be writing about yourself — although at some unconscious level you always are. What I mean is that you are the subject and your pen is sovereign. If you let it, that pen will carry you on an extraordinary journey of discovery. If you let go and surrender to the journey, you will find yourself writing flowingly and freely, letting the sentences of your story unfold without your conscious mind getting in the way.

Continue to write on the Muse Stream for at least twenty minutes; make it thirty or forty-five, if you can...sixty, if you dare.

Remember to write without stopping, to write without editing or correcting, to write without thinking or censoring. To go with first thoughts. To write without judging. Write until you feel complete. Then write for ten minutes more.

After You've Written

What did you discover from your writing? About your story? About your creative process? Did continuing for those additional ten minutes reveal something unexpected? About you? About your story? About your creative process?

Trust. Let Go. Leap.

Legendary science fiction author Ray Bradbury once said that, for him, writing was about leaping off cliffs and trusting that he would sprout wings on the way down. In many ways, what Bradbury describes is the way of the Fool in the tarot: that surrendered leap of faith into the void that alchemically transforms into art something that, in the moment, appears to make no sense.

Life is like that too. Why wouldn't it be when, as I continue to point out in these pages, the precepts of one apply equally to the other, when the first "rule" of both is that there are no rules?

Not only do I do my best to write that way, I do my best to live that way. It's sometimes terrifying, but ultimately satisfying. And even though it means living and writing without a net, those wings Bradbury talks about have never failed to appear.

They first showed themselves to me in a dream I had three decades ago. In it, I was clinging to the roof ledge of a 1950's-style high-rise while an inner voice kept urging me to jump. I didn't dare...I couldn't. And, as with the dream I shared with you about the garage attendant in "Making Friends with Your Inner Critic" (Section 8), I woke up frightened and upset.

As I did with other dream, I took this image into meditation. Unfortunately, this experience was not as immediately successful as would be its successor. In each of three sessions, I tried to release my grip on that old structure and failed. By the fourth, I was so uncomfortable that I just did it. I unhooked my fingers from the stonework in my mind, fully expecting to plummet to the pavement in a messy splat.

Unlike Bradbury, I didn't sprout wings. Instead, I found myself floating gently, feather-like, until I landed in what I could only then describe as the arms of God.

Before he died, Apple's Steve Jobs said, "You have to trust in something — your gut, destiny, life, karma, whatever. This approach has never let me down, and it has made all the difference in my life."

Jobs was right. That "something" has never let me down. Over the years, in both my writing and my life, I have made many moves and done many risky things that defy logic and convention. And although I have experienced fear and discomfort along the way, the ultimate rewards have far outweighed the fallout.

Through all that, I have discovered that once I commit to the highest possible path and purpose, a trinity of principles is always at play:

Trust
Let Go
Leap

First, I trust the voice of my deepest heart, which is also the voice of my highest imperative and my Muse — the voice of what I sometimes call "infinite mind" or my "wisest self."

Next, I let go of all resistance, all clinging and all clutching (which does not mean that I'm not afraid and which also does not mean that I have to know how whatever I'm being called to do is possible).

Finally, I leap into the void — like that Fool in the tarot.

I do it on the page, and I do it in my life. And when I do, miracles always follow. Always.

Miracles are present not only in my life. Miracles are present in every life. In every moment of every life — and in every moment of every creative life. It's our limited vision that prevents us from seeing them. It's our limited sense of what is possible that prevents us from believing in them. It's our fear that prevents us from embracing them.

Trust. Let Go. Leap. In my writing as in my life, it always works.

Exploration

Writing is an act of pilgrimage. We set out on a journey, intent on a direction and destination. Yet if we are true to our art and to our heart, we free the story to carry us where it will. The resulting journey is one that reveals to us not only the story we are writing, but the story we are living.

When we listen for the stories that move through us, we also discover the story that is us. How has your writing been a pilgrimage? What has it taught you — about yourself, about your work, about the world? Write about that without thinking too deeply about it. Instead, let the Muse Stream reveal to you what you didn't know you knew.

You Are a Writer

A Guided Meditation

I include this meditation in all my books for writers because it is too easy, as creative artists working largely in isolation, to diminish both ourselves and our output and to forget that we are powerful and empowered creators.

Listen to this meditation when you feel doubt...when you feel less-than...when you don't believe that you will ever be able to complete your writing project...when you question whether you are even a writer. In those moments, let the words and spirit of this meditation remind you that you are a writer — of power, passion, strength and courage. For writing is an act of courage... of immeasurable courage. And you are doing it!

∫ ∫ ∫

Allow 5 minutes for this meditative experience

My studio recording of this meditation is available for download or streaming as part "The Voice of the Muse Companion: Guided Meditations for Writers." See "Guided Meditations" in Section 1 ("Getting Started") to find out how to access the recording, as well as for tips on how best to use this book's meditations.

Close your eyes and take a few deep breaths as you relax and listen...

You are a writer. You are a writer of power, passion, strength and, yes, courage. For writing is an act of courage. Acknowledge that courage, the courage that got you to this point...having written. Having written today, if you have. Having written just now, if you have. Having written at some point during your experience with this book.

You are a writer. Breathe into that. Breathe into the release you felt as the pen flowed across the page, as letters formed into words, words stretched into sentences and sentences began to fill your pages.

Breathe into the freedom, the vibrancy, the love. Breathe into the knowledge and knowingness that you can do it again. And again. And again. And again.

You are a writer. What you write is powerful. What you write is vibrant. What you write, whatever you believe in this moment, is luminous.

Trust that to the best of your ability, in this moment. Acknowledge the writer you are, in this moment. Breathe into that.

Breathe out judgment. Breathe out fear. Breathe out not-good-enoughs. Breathe out comparisons. What others have written does not matter. What you have written is all that matters now, in this moment. It is perfect...in this moment. Know that. Trust that.

Breathe into that.

If you don't feel ready to read what you have written from that place of trust, discernment and compassion, set it aside. Set it aside for a time — until you arrive at a place of more clarity, more objectivity, more self-love.

Don't avoid reading it, but nor need you rush into it. Either way, for now, know that you are a writer. A writer writes. That's what you have done. You have written.

You are a *writer*.

You *are* a writer.

You are a writer.

You've heard the words. Now speak them with me...

I am a *writer*.

I *am* a writer.

I am a writer.

Speak them again and again and again, knowing them to be true.
Speak them again, feeling the truth in them.
Speak them again, for they are true.

14. Before You Go...

What do dreams know of boundaries?
AMELIA EARHART

Only those who risk going too far can possibly find out how far they can go.
T.S. ELIOT

Leaps of Faith

We enter into this lifetime in the leap of faith that our soul takes into the being in our mother's womb. We take that one huge leap only to discover that such leaps never cease being demanded of us.

First one leap into the unknown, then another, then another, then another, until that instant when with our final breath, we take the ultimate leap of faith…into the unknowable.

Each leap represents a greater risk. Each leap challenges us more profoundly. Yet each leap on the path to that ultimate one opens us to greater miracles and richer rewards.

And with each of those leaps, we feel more alive, more in the flow and more aligned with our heart's desire and our soul's passion.

Always.

Are you ready to take your next leap of faith? Are you ready to trust, let go and leap…onto the page…into your life?

"What if I fail?" I hear you ask.

What if you don't?

It's Time to Live the Dream

A Guided Meditation

Allow at least 15 minutes for this meditative experience and for the writing that flows from it.

Settle into a quiet, comfortable place where you won't be disturbed for fifteen or twenty minutes. Close your eyes, relax and focus on your breath — breathing in and out, in and out, in and out...slowly, deeply... then more slowly, more deeply.

Let your breath dissolve all the cares and worries of your day, all the distractions that keep you from focusing on your most heartfelt dreams for your writing. Breathe into your heart, that central brain that knows all and fears nothing, that is the source of all, that is the dwelling place of all your deepest desires...your soul's desire and imperative...your hopes, dreams and passions. Your stories.

Without thinking, just surrendering to whatever first bubbles up into your awareness, answer the following question. Remember to not second-guess yourself or censor yourself, and remember to go with first thoughts. Always first thoughts.

What's my dream for my writing? For my writing self?

Remember: No thinking, no analyzing. Whatever comes up first, whether or not it seems to make conventional sense or seems possible to realize.

Again...

What's my dream for my writing? For my writing self?

Take a moment to journal your answer, then continue with the meditation.

Were you surprised by what came up? Was it something you have long suspected? Was it something you have always known? Or was it something that, until this moment, you had no conscious awareness of?

Know that whatever it is, however improbable it may seem in this moment, it's not impossible.

Nearly every success story begins with an "impossible" dream. Nearly every "overnight success" was years in the making.

So, what about your writing dreams? Have you abandoned them? Stuffed them in the back of a drawer because they seem so unreachable?

Open that drawer. Reach your hand in. Gently. Touch it. Reconnect with it. Reconnect with yourself.

Have you started the book you have always seen yourself writing? The screenplay or stage play? The cycle of poems? The short story? The song? The essay or blog post?

No?

Then now is the time to take steps to put your dream into action. It doesn't matter whether you can give it five minutes a day or five hours. It doesn't even matter whether you know in this moment what it's about or where it will take you.

Every journey begins with a single step. Every piece of writing begins with a single word. One word. Any word.

Write that word. Now.

Open your heart again. Open your heart to the vision. Open your heart to yourself.

Open your heart to your life. Say *yes* to you!

Try This

Write on the Muse Stream from the phrase "I am ready to live my writing dream…" If you know what your writing dreams are, let this be a statement of commitment and part of your first step in realizing them. If you don't, let yourself discover dreams you never knew you had through this exploration.

Try This Too

Also on the Muse Stream, take the word that came to you in the meditation and, surrendering to it and to every word that follows, free your writing dreams to take shape on the page. Be the writer you are.

Endings and Beginnings

Promise me you'll always remember: You're braver
than you believe, and stronger than you seem,
and smarter than you think.

A.A. Milne

...a writer is a writer because even when there is no hope, even
when nothing you do shows any sign of promise,
you keep writing anyway.

Junot Díaz

Remember the first exercise I asked you to do, in "Preparing to Flow Forward"? I invited you to initiate a *Writer's Block Unblocked* journal by jotting down where you were (or weren't) in your writing as you joined me on this journey into your creative reawakening. Then I urged you to avoid looking over those inaugural writings until you had finished this book.

You have finished, and it's time. Open your journal to those early pages and first thoughts. Read them. Reintroduce yourself to the blocked writer you believed yourself to have been last week...last month...last year...whenever it was you began working with this book.

- Do you recognize the writer you were?
- Are you surprised now by what you wrote then?
- Has anything changed?
- Has everything changed?

Now, open to a blank page in your *Writer's Block Unblocked* journal. Close your eyes, take a few deep breaths and whisk yourself back in time...back to the day you first opened this book...back to the day you wrote those words.

As you continue to focus on your breath, allow yourself to journey forward from that day to this one. Review and relive all you experienced through that time, recalling fears and flowering, terrors and triumphs.

Let those feeling-memories swirl through you for a few moments. Then, taking another few deep breaths, allow a single word, phrase or sentence to bubble up into your conscious awareness, one that describes where you are in this moment of endings and new beginnings. Don't judge it. Don't censor it. Don't second-guess it. Surrender to it, whatever it is, then write it under today's date next to the question, "Where am I now?"

Now, on the Muse Stream, write a few lines describing where you are today with your writing.

- What did you accomplish and achieve over the course of our time together?
- What has changed since you wrote those first words all those pages ago?
- Where are you at the end of this book that you weren't at the beginning? That you couldn't imagine being at the beginning?
- Where do you choose to go from here? With your writing? With your life? With your dreams?

Wherever that is, take your first step toward that goal.
Do it.
Now.
You *are* a writer!

Share the Journey

I would love to hear about your experiences moving from stuckness to creative flow, as well as about your writing dreams and the steps you are now taking to realize them.

To that end, I invite you to share your stories about your creative journey on www.markdavidgerson.com/yourstories. What you post on this private page will not be shared publicly unless you give me explicit permission to do so, with or without your name. If you are open to having me post all or part of your contribution — in my newsletter and/or on social media — also include your work's title and a purchase link, if you have one.

While I can't promise to respond to or post every submission, I will read them all and get back to you wherever possible. I look forward with great anticipation to hearing from you.

Meantime, good luck...and write on!

Gratitude

I have never sought out the books I have written. Rather, they have always sought me out, often with tricksterish glee. Sometimes, to make certain I pay attention, they have employed human messengers to attract my notice. That was the case with *Writer's Block Unblocked*, which would not exist today had Aalia Kazan not suggested it and had Kathleen Messmer not urged me forward with it. I am grateful to both for their unconditional and unqualified support over the years, as I am to Joan Cerio and Sander Freedman, who have tirelessly urged me on — with this and many of my creative projects over the years.

Additional appreciation goes to Kathleen Messmer for this new edition's evocative cover image and for the author portrait on the back cover.

Thanks, too, must go to Carole H. Leckner, whose forceful compassion three decades ago helped chip away the first chunks of my own writer's block.

As much as I learned much from Carole, I have learned even more from those I have mentored, coached and taught. I thank them all for levels of courage, commitment, drive and heart-discipline that continue to inspire me. I also acknowledge the many online friends I have never met in person who have cheered me on — on this project as on many others.

Writing can be a solitary and sometimes lonely pursuit. One way I deal with this is by writing in cafés. It can help me feel engaged with the public world even as I withdraw into my private one. For the original edition of this book, I owe a debt of gratitude to the baristas of various Starbucks outlets in Albuquerque, who always made me feel welcome in my writing-home-away-from-home.

The energy of place has informed all my writing projects. Just as each draft of each book or screenplay tells me which music to listen to, whether to drink tea (Irish breakfast) or coffee (my version of an Americano) and what time of day to write, it also moves me around North America to meet its requirements. I have written all or parts of various of my completed works in two Canadian provinces and countless U.S. states. Astoundingly, *Writer's Block Unblocked* owes a direct debt to only two of those locales: Albuquerque, where I wrote the first edition, and Sedona, where this revised and expanded edition was conceived and completed. I remain grateful to both for their inspiration, most particularly to the Sandia Mountains that soar up from Albuquerque's eastern flanks and to the red rocks of Sedona, which, however often I leave them, keep calling me back.

I would be remiss if I failed to include a profound expression of gratitude to the long-ago retired MacBook Pro upon which I typed the initial drafts of the first edition of *Writer's Block Unblocked*. It soldiered on valiantly, years past retirement age, contributing to this and many other of my writing projects its tenacity, resolve and fortitude, and reminding me of those same, too-often overlooked qualities in myself.

Finally, as always, to my Muse and to the presence of Story in my life: As life-giving as the air I breathe, the water I drink and the food I eat, they nourish, nurture and sustain me in ways that nothing else can. *Mahalo.*

More Writing Inspiration!

The Legend of Q'ntana

"Epic Adventures Rich with Universal Truth!"

Soon to Be a Series of Major Motion Pictures!

www.ingramcontent.com/pod-product-compliance
Lightning Source LLC
Chambersburg PA
CBHW030316100526
44592CB00010B/451